GW00703343

by
Pat Davis

Geerings of Ashford Ltd.,
Ashford, Kent, England.

Kent
People and Places

Geerings of Ashford Ltd.,
Ashford, Kent, England

First published 1997

ISBN 1 873953 30 5

*Designed and printed by
Geerings of Ashford Ltd., Ashford, Kent, England.*

Contents

ABBOT, George, Archbishop of Canterbury 1

ADAMS, Will 2

ALPHEGE 3

ANNE OF CLEVES 4

ASTOR, John Jacob Jnr 6

ASTOR, 1st Viscount William Waldorf of Hever Castle .. 7

BABBINGTON, Margaret 11

BACCELLI, Giannetta 12

BENNETT, Joseph 13

BLOUNT, Richard 13

BLUE, Little Bit of 15

CAESAR, Julius 15

CAUSEY, Belle 18

CHURCHILL, Sir Winston Leonard Spencer 18

COOPER, Thomas Sydney 21

COURTENAY, Sir William 23

CULMER, Richard 25

CUSHING, Peter 26

DADD, Richard 27

'DISGUSTED' OF TUNBRIDGE WELLS 29

DUNSTAN, Saint 30

EDWARD, THE BLACK PRINCE 31

GELDOF, Bob, K.B.E. 33

GERMAIN, Lady Elizabeth ('Betty') 34

GORDON, Charles George, General 35

GREAT DUNSTAN 36

HARRYS, Richard 37

HARVEY, William 38

HEATH, Edward R. G. 40

HENGIST - AND HORSA 41

HOWLEY, Dr William, Archbishop of Canterbury 42

JAGGER, Mick 44

JEZREEL, James Jershom 44

JOY, Richard 46

KITCHENER, Horatio Herbert, 1st Earl Kitchener of Khartoum
         46

LANFRANC   49

MYNN, Alfred   51

NAPOLEON, Louis, Emperor of France   52

NASH, Richard (Beau)   55

ODO, Bishop of Bayeux, Earl of Kent   57

PAGE, Geoffrey, D.S.O., D.F.C. and Bar, O.B.E.   58

PETO, Sir Samuel Morton Bart, M.P.   59

PETT, Phineas   60

PITT, William, The Elder; 1st Earl of Chatham   62

PITT, William, The Younger   63

PLUTO   65

POCAHONTAS   66

PUGIN, Augustus Welby Northmore   67

RANSLEY, George   68

ROSE, Sir Alec   70

SHIRLEY, Doctor John   72

SHOVELL, Sir Clowdisley   74

SICKERT, Walter   75

SNOB   76

STANHOPE, Charles, 3rd Earl Stanhope   77

STANHOPE, Lady Hester Lucy   78

STUART, Frances   79

Dr. SYN   80

THORNDIKE, Dame Sybil   81

THORNTON, Charles Inglis   82

TULLIS, Julie   84

TYLER, Wat   84

WEBB, Captain Matthew   86

WELLINGTON, Arthur Wellesley, 1st Duke of Wellington ..   88

WILLES, John   91

WOLFE, James   91

ZBOROWSKI, Count Vorow   94

Dedication

THIS book is enthusiastically dedicated to my P. A., my long standing and long suffering wife, Pat.

Without her dynamic drive this book might never have been completed.

Thanks, Pat!

ABBOT, George, Archbishop of Canterbury (1562-1633)

Abysmal Archer . . .

W as it a sign of ecclesiastical greatness to come that he had so humble a cradle as a damp riverside cottage that later became a low tavern, 'The Three Mariners' in Guildford?

His mother, when pregnant, certainly had a dream which prophesied it. If a jack jumped into her pail when next she filled her pitcher with water from the stream, she knew her son would do great things. And sure enough, John Aubrey, who tells a good tale, assures us that one did just that.

George's father, a cloth cutter, could not afford an Oxford springboard for his son but his godparents, taking their baptismal vows seriously, dipped deep into their pockets for his education. With his degree achieved, George developed so strict a Puritanism that he had religious pictures burnt in the market-place.

By the time he was 50, he had risen through the ecclesiastical ranks to become Archbishop of Canterbury. He detested both Pope and Popery so heartily that he tried to foment war with ardently Catholic Spain. Even so, perhaps he too yearned for infallibility for he hated any contradiction and draconianly suppressed all ideas which he disliked 'by excessive harshness'.

Biographers of his day described him as 'sometimes choleric'. But it was in no fit of wild rage that, in 1611, Archbishop became assassin. Totally unaware that he was no William Tell, he had jumped at the chance of a break from his ecclesiastical duties when Lord Zouch invited him to join a hunting party on his estate. The host, for his part, was under no misapprehension as to the Archbishop's failing, and warned fellow guests and beaters alike of it. Despite this, one of the latter, Peter Hawkins, sadly strayed into his line of fire . . .

The Archbishop was so greatly distressed that he immediately settled £20 a year on his grieving widow. No great sum perhaps for the loss of a husband in his prime but it was enough for her to speedily procure another. There was some balm too for the Archbishop's wounded soul. James I, no less, insisted 'No one but a fool or a knave can blame you'. The jury too were on his side to a man: 'Per infortinium suae propria culpae' or in modern parlance, 'his (the gamekeeper's) own silly fault.'

Unfortunately, there's always a Devil's advocate. In this case it was John Williams, Bishop-elect for Lincoln, who stirred up trouble. Homicide, he resolutely maintained, made the Archbishop 'irregular' . . . surely also liable to the forfeiture of his estate. So 'irregular' indeed did the good Bishop consider his Archbishop that he stoutly refused to be consecrated by such an evil man. Commissions of Enquiry were held then as regularly, lengthily and doubtlessly as expensively as now. Again,

1

the Archbishop was cleared; his high office left unsullied. For all that, the event 'cast him into deep shadow for the rest of his life'.

On his death, however, he was remembered for his many generous benefactions rather than for his single lethal lapse with a crossbow. One benefaction (how history repeats itself!) was 'to find work for the younger sort of people'.

ADAMS, Will (1564-1620)

Father of the Japanese Navy . . .

IT was a good day for the Japanese when Will Adams was born in Gillingham; a still better one for them when, aged 12, he was apprenticed to a Thames boatbuilder.

From such small beginnings . . . By the time he was 24 he was sailing munitions and provisions in his own 120 ton vessel to Drake and his captains as they ceaselessly harried the Armada making heavy going up-Channel.

In 1598 he had a much bigger command. He had been appointed Pilot Major of a five-strong Dutch fleet hoping to get their share of rich trading with the East. For him it was a rare opportunity to amass wealth - but it meant leaving his wife and child, Deliverance . . . 'Three or four years at most' he hazarded consolingly.

Wind, wave and weather, however, had other ideas. Contrary gales swept him hopelessly off course in the South Atlantic . . . and forced him to winter on the bleak shores of the Magellan Strait. Came the Spring, and only three ships headed out across the Pacific. And only one, Adam's own, the 'Charity', found harbour at Bungo in Japan.

This first ever Englishman was received with scant hospitality. At the instigation of jealous Jesuits and Portuguese traders he was lodged in prison. Even when released from captivity he was still a virtual prisoner, one too valuable to be allowed his freedom. The Japanese, shrewd then as now, desperately wanted to learn Western shipbuilding skills much more than they wanted trade. So, two boats later, now the confidant of Emperor Iyeyasu, he was honoured as Chief Pilot; awarded a pension, and the status of a Samurai: he was 'favoured as never before had been any Christian in those parts of the world'.

'Living like a lord in England' he was given estates, servants . . . and women. Bigamy presumably was no crime - and temptation was too great. Deliverance was never to see her father again!

Later, Adams sailed to Siam and Cochin China and in 1613 did set up a trading post. He died in 1620 and Japan lived in mercantile isolation until

1853 when Commodore Perry and his warships rather pointedly suggested that trade with the rest of the world would be no bad thing. Little did he know . . .

Japan celebrated Adams' tercentenary with the erection of a statue in Tokyo; Gillingham with a more modest clock-tower beside the main Thanet-London road. The whole dramatic story is the basis of James Clavell's intriguing 'Shogun'.

ALPHEGE (954-1012)

Saint - and Martyr . . .

ONCE a hermit, near Bath, he rose to become Archbishop of Canterbury so following in the spiritual steps of his one-time mentor, Dunstan.

His early life was a model of asceticism; one that he never forgot. It was said that when he was Bishop of Winchester there were no beggars in the streets because of his open-handed generosity. Generous with his money, but frugal with his meals, constant fasting made him so thin that when, at the altar, he raised his hands on high to God, his flock swore they could see clearly through them.

Undoubtedly frail in body: but equally staunch in spirit. When the Vikings, under Thorkill the Tall and Olaf the Stout (unforgetful of the St Brice's Day massacre in which host had treacherously murdered guest) fell upon Canterbury in 1011, Alphege refused to flee to safety. And when, through the treachery of the Abbot of neighbouring St Augustine's, to whom he had once been too merciful, the City was forced to surrender after a 20 days' siege, he implored the berserk warriors, 'Turn your fury on me' as with cold-blooded impartiality they massacred not only men but women and children as well. He was forced too to watch his monks stumble out of the Cathedral, set ablaze like a torch by flaring barrels of tar, only to be ruthlessly hacked down when they thought they had evaded death.

Equally staunchly, he refused to let church money be given to pay his own ransom to the clamouring Vikings: 'All I can give you is the Word of God'. Infuriated by his stubbornness, his enemies shackled him, then half-led, half-dragged him like an animal from camp to camp. Seven months later, near Greenwich, during an orgy, an ox-bone was thrown at him in drunken contempt. And was followed by a murderous fusilade of still more heavy bones. At last one of his converts took pity on him and, with his battle-axe, put the old man out of his agony.

Alphege's broken body was taken to London, not to give it decent burial there but to demand a ransom be paid, if not in life, then in death. That done, St Paul's monks reverently interred it.

Then, some ten years later, came a Viking with a conscience! Canute, son of Svein Forkbeard. Canute was not only the Danish king but also, after defeating Edmund Ironside in battle; murdering every possible claimant to the throne; and forcing the widow of Edmund's predecessor to marry him, King of the English too. And a murderous heathen had turned Christian (1016).

In penitence, he gave the people of Kent, the country's most prosperous port, Sandwich, and with it all the harbour dues. It was the same Sandwich where only a few years before he had casually dumped hostages ashore, hostages with hands, noses and ears hacked off!

Yet despite such barbarity, he ruled his two countries wisely and well; and had Alphege's body disinterred. With his own hands he steered the ornate royal barge bearing it across the Thames so that it might thence be taken for burial to Canterbury. So 'with much majesty and bliss he was brought gloriously into the Cathedral' to be placed on the north side of the altar next to Dunstan.

As a final gesture of contrition, Canute himself came to the Cathedral to give his crown to the monks, 'to do with as they would'. Triumphantly, they hung it from the Great Rood Screen high above the Nave altar. A fitting gesture by a Lord Temporal to a Lord Spiritual.

ANNE OF CLEVES (1517-1557)

A Flemish Mare . . .

SUCH was Henry VIII's horrified assessment of the young woman whom, unseen, he had contracted to marry - purely for diplomatic reasons. With France and Spain in alliance after his breach with Rome, and with his divorce of Catherine of Aragon, he needed allies. Any ally - at any price.

Holbein, sent to the German principality of Cleves as 'Court Photographer', must have been torn between artistic and diplomatic truth. He softened her tall angularity and toned down the pockmarked face though he could do nothing to tone down her gutteral German accent. Henry, fooled perhaps by this portrait, found her in the flesh to be 'Well and seemly but not so fair as reported'. She was certainly far from Henry's idea of 'beddable'.

But she was to have her moments . . . At Calais, in 1540, where she had to wait impatiently for a fair wind she was cheered and fêted. At

Dover, she was greeted by the Duke of Suffolk and lodged in the castle's Royal Apartments. At Canterbury it was the Archbishop and four of his Suffragans. There 300 men had worked day and night for two months to build royal apartments for her by the Great Court in St Augustine's Abbey. Huge charcoal-filled braziers had glowed ceaselessly to dry them out. All for a single night! At Rochester, the Duke of Norfolk welcomed her.

And at Greenwich - in grand climax - it was the King himself. Both dressed in cloth of gold, they rode to the Palace through ranks of gentlemen in black velvet with gold chains round their necks, and were greeted by the Mayor of London in crimson velvet.

They were married on Twelfth Night. Jousting at Court and processions on the Thames marked the great occasion. Their wedding night however was far from spectacular. Next day, eagerly quizzed by her curious ladies-in-waiting, Anne unabashedly described it all: 'When he comes to bed . . . he kisses me . . . takes me by the hand . . . and biddeth me "Goodnight, Sweet Heart"'. Puzzled by their astounded faces she queried 'Is that not enough?'. In her extraordinary innocence, a child could be created by a kiss.

Even before his marriage Henry had stormed at his cringeing Chancellor, 'Am I to put my neck into such a noose?' Now, although he had not even tasted the fruit he was appalled: 'I liked her not well before but now much worse'.

Ever a man of roughshod action he was already testing the possibilities of Norfolk's niece, flirtatious Catherine Howard. Unknown to him she had had two youthful, passionate affairs, one of which she was disastrously to renew during a rejuvenated Henry's Royal Progress.

Flanders mare or no, Anne fainted in womanly anguish when news of Parliament's annulment of their marriage (trust Henry to shift the blame) was broken to her. But £3,000 and 100 manors (of which Dartford and Anne Boleyn's Hever Castle were to become her favourites) did much to assuage her battered pride. After all, was she not henceforward to be the King's Sister? Later she was to ride in high state beside Elizabeth at Queen Mary's coronation. And on the latter's specific instructions, she was honoured by burial in Westminster Abbey - beneath a marble slab costing £7 - and decorated with the skull and crossbones!

No, life was not too bad for Anne of Cleves. As willing a trencherman as Henry she feasted well and often. Even had royal doggie bags: capacious pockets in her dresses which she stuffed with delicacies far too good to be wasted.

ASTOR, John Jacob Jnr (1886-1971)

Millionaire Who Made Good . . .

BORN with a golden spoon in his mouth and heir to Hever Castle, J.J. was not content to sit back on his wealth. He made his mark as a soldier, business man - and eventually proprietor of "The Times".

He was eight when his mother died; 13 when his father renounced America and became an English citizen. Eton was not merely a jumping-off point for him but one which he long remembered with great affection. Oxford, New College, of course followed - but only briefly.

Briefly, because he soon found that academic life did not stretch him. He preferred practicality in the Army: initially amid the glamour of the First Life Guards, then in the even more glamorous Household Cavalry. In the former he had a spell as aide-de-camp with a near neighbour, a man associated with an equally famous Kent mansion, Lord Hardinge of Penshurst Place; Viceroy of India. But there was certainly no glamour for J.J. in the Great War of 1914-18. Wounded at Messines, he brusquely refused the cushy Staff appointments offered him. Instead he plunged into bloody action again . . . won the Legion of Honour medal . . . and was wounded in the last months of the war.

Not even the hardiest leg can survive 14 pieces of jagged shrapnel in it. It had to go. To be replaced by an artificial limb. Not an expensive bang-up-to-the-minute job but a Tommy's run-of-the-mill 'tin leg'. And, he insisted, it must be made in a British Legion workshop.

Air-ace Douglas Bader lost two legs, and after falling flat on his face untold times, mastered golf. So too did rather luckier J.J. In addition he played cricket - tennis - and he even won the Parliamentary Squash Rackets Championship!

Obviously he was not a man to let the loss of a leg plunge him into apathy and depression. But, to make doubly certain, to give him a demanding new interest, his father put magnificent Hever Castle and its huge estate into his hands just as he had given equally magnificent Cliveden, on the Thames, to his elder brother. J.J. loved the place though not perhaps with his father's all-consuming intensity.

But he was deeply moved by the gesture. Moved too when a Household Cavalry standard was laid up in Hever Church - near the tomb of gross and graceless Thomas Bullen. Moved too when he was made Deputy Lord Lieutenant of Kent, a Justice of the Peace, and an Honorary Colonel of the Kent Heavy Brigade, R.A.

Much though he enjoyed Hever and country life in Kent, it was not enough to satisfy his deep sense of duty, his wish to play a worthwhile part in English affairs. Iron principled, a man of integrity who never went back on his word, he and his name were much in demand when distinguished company directors were needed on the Board of important companies. He was elected Unionist MP for Dover but was never a fluent speaker.

Greater fulfilment came when Lord Northcliffe died. There was panic at Times House as they debated on his successor. Finally one of the anxious hierarchy remembered a very wealthy but equally modest undergraduate he had once met at Oxford. An undergraduate wealthy enough to buy 'The Thunderer' and keep it afloat through financial storms; and yet one modest enough to leave the actual thundering to those who knew best.

J.J. did buy a major share in 'The Times'. But it was only after firmly laying down the guidelines, more firmly than Lord Northcliffe had ever done, to John Walter, the current editor, that he left day to day policy entirely in the hands of each of the latter's four succesors.

For all his wealth, J.J. was a man of great self-discipline who lived unostentatiously. Gifts totalling over a million pounds were quietly passed to the Middlesex Hospital as a heartfelt thank-you for the medical care he had received when his leg was amputated. Marriage to the Earl of Minto's daughter brought him out from his quiet shell - and Hever parties once again became great occasions.

Sadly, he was driven from Hever, Kent and England by punitive taxation. The huge Astor Trust Funds in America built up by his great-grandfather had brought wealth into England, the country whose traditions J.J. loved and upheld. Reluctantly, not only for his own sake but also for that of the many dependent on his generosity and investment, he had to emigrate to the South of France.

There he died at Cannes.

ASTOR, 1st Viscount William Waldorf of Hever Castle (1848-1919)

Visionary Viscount . . .

W. W. was a rarity - a Yank who preferred English citizenship to American; and the tranquillity of Kent to the bustle of New York. But then he could afford to, couldn't he?

His great-grandfather, John Jacob Astor (1763-1848) had been a man of unusual character too. And to know him is to understand W.W. the better. Son of a poor but convivial butcher, J.J. had somehow scraped up

7

passage-money, enough to take him, in 1783, from the backwoods village of Waldorf, near Heidelberg, to booming Baltimore, U.S.A.

There, using an innate business sense, he sold a chance consignment of silver flutes to such profitable advantage that, by the time he was 22, he had built up a monopoly of the Great Lakes fur trade. With ships a drug on the market in war-torn Europe, he bought up a veritable fleet of them.

In them he shipped his furs - and on one occasion, opium - to China; and Chinese goods to America. It was a double whammy long before its time. And, just to improve the day, he had invested shrewdly in New York real estate - to become the wealthiest man in the Land of the Free, a man with a hundred million dollars to pass down to his descendants.

An only child, W.W. trained in Columbia Law School and ran, unsuccessfully, for Congress and for Governor of New York State but to such good effect that, in 1884, President Chester appointed him Minister to Italy. It was a post that, owing to the vagaries of American politics lasted only three years. Short time though it was, it was long enough for him to acquire a sizeable amount of Ancient Rome which he dearly loved.

So, in 1890, back not to America which he openly despised (and which, in turn, mercilessly lampooned him) but to England which he much admired. In particular to that rare jewel of house and garden, Cliveden (1893) with its breathtaking view down one of the loveliest reaches of the Thames. To make perfection even more perfect he added an entire balustrade from Rome's famous Villa Borghese. And at the entrance to the rhododendron-flanked drive he placed a specially commissioned Fountain of Love. On it, three shapely ladies, each with her cheeky Cupid, lounged languidly round the edge of a huge scallop shell of gleaming white, Verona marble. That done, he gave Cliveden to his eldest son - as a wedding present!

In 1901, emulating Caesar, he had come to Hever Castle in Kent; he had seen . . . but it was he who had been conquered by its rich historical associations with Anne Boleyn, and by the moated castle itself. Two years later, when it came on the market, it was his turn to conquer. He snapped it up, together with a trifling matter of 640 acres of gardens and parkland; and the very important one of the hand of Mary Paul of Philadelphia!

That, of course, was only the beginning. W.W. was still American enough to want 20th century comfort, not medieval privation. And although he was said to be austere and unloveable, he had, as multi-millionaires obviously have, many friends eager for his hospitality. So the interior was discreetly modernised and embellished with the finest panelling and works of art: Titian and Holbein . . . Clouet and Cranach . . . And the entire exterior was repointed simply because the cement was comparatively modern - and not to Tudor specification! W.W., like J.J., was meticulous to a degree.

Guests presented a slightly larger problem but one far from insoluble. He couldn't tinker about adding piecemeal extensions to a splendid Tudor mansion. So, in the finest tradition of American enterprise, why not build an entire 20th century Tudor village - with its own power station - just across the moat. Which is precisely what W.W. did - even the chimneys were all different, copies of those at Hampton Court. A few other minor alterations had to be made before he could set to work on the gardens. The River Eden had to be driven back a hundred yards to prevent flooding. And for the same reason the whole Castle had to have a common or garden damp-proof, asphalt floor; on top of it seasoned oak was laid on fine pine.

* * * * *

Pause for a moment before we start work on the gardens. In 1892, W.W. had founded the Liberal Pall Mall Gazette - later spent a million or two more on purchasing 'The Observer' (1911). Not as a permanent business trophy but solely to ensure that the sitting Editor, J. L. Garvin could become editor of The Gazette. And in 1899, perhaps with a presentiment that he was to own some of England's finest heritage, he became a naturalised English citizen.

* * * * *

W.W. did not believe in half measures. In 1903 his total work force shot up to 1,000 when he decided that 35 acres of rather boggy land would look vastly better if he diverted the River Eden into it to create a lake. A lake between 5 and 10 feet deep, some half mile in length, and complete with weir, sluice-gates and 100' long cast-iron pipe-subway under the Eden! It was a mammoth task but one which, with the help of 800 men, 16 diggers, and 7 miles of railway, was completed, in 1906, after beavering work by day and, when necessary, by night. As a finishing touch, at its west end, he built a colonnaded piazza, not unworthy of Rome.

With experts, W.W. planned and supervised everything. He thought big. He was prepared to put his money where his mouth was. Obviously such a lake demanded equally impressive landscape gardens. So he ordered attack on a second front by more men, more steam diggers - and cranes. Cranes? Why cranes? Because some trees having been ill-placed by Nature had to be re-planted more artistically by Waldorf.

And when there were insufficient of them to make the perfect picture, towering Scots pines were brought 12 miles from Ashdown Forest on long drays hauled by six straining horses, with ten sweating men in attendance. Soil too had to be imported or shifted to give the sleekest contours. Giant rocks were brought in from Chiddingstone Causeway to create the rockery.

W.W. certainly had an eye for beauty. A thousand dark yews were planted to make a Maze. Hundreds more, golden ones; were skilfully sculptured into giant chessmen. Then there were also the Half Moon Pond, Rhododendron Walk, balustraded Golden Stairs, Smugglers' Way,

Splashwater, Rose Garden, Waterfalls . . . and, of course, Anne Boleyn's Walk. But most beautiful of all were the golden sandstone-walled Italian Gardens, richly enhanced by Roman statutary and sculpture; sarcophagi and well-heads; columns of Imperial porphry, bronze vases, Pompeian pottery jars and Venetian lions . . .

W.W.'s well deserved elevation to Baron and then to Viscount (1917) for large gifts to War charities, did not receive from his son the acclaim a father might have expected. As MP for Plymouth, the young man recognised that, on his father's death, he would have to move from Commons to Lords - so ending his high hopes of political advancement. It was indeed a blow for him!

But not for the nation. For his lively and inexperienced American wife, Nancy, stepped readily into the breach: campaigned flamboyantly: 'If you want a Party Hack, *don't* vote for me'. And was elected (for 25 years!) with a 5,000 majority to become the first woman ever to grace the House of Commons.

And grace it she certainly did with her personal magnetism, sharp wit, and intelligence. With her passionate demands for the rights of women and children, she showed some 650 males that she was far from being an easy, feminine pushover. Her equally passionate demands for virtual prohibition were however met with polite derision. No respecter of persons, she dared to say to Winston Churchill, 'If I were your wife, I would put poison in your coffee.' And for once received even better than she gave, 'If I were your husband I'ld gladly drink it'.

William Waldorf Astor had wrought miracles. He had endowed Kent with the finest castle and gardens in the South of England . . . In all England? And in creating them, the Anglo-American great-grandson of the German butcher's son, now a fully fledged Englishman, had probably spent more money than any other man since Nebuchadnezzar had built the Hanging Gardens of Babylon for his wife.

* * * * *

In 1995, Hever Castle won the Historic Houses Association's Garden of the Year Award.

BABBINGTON, Margaret (1878-1958)

True Friend of a Cathedral . . .

SHE must surely have been the first person to pass St Peter at the portals of Heaven on a bicycle. Her machine was better known in Canterbury than the Lord Mayor's car. She rode it everywhere; rode it until growing infirmity (hers!) forced her finally to dismount. During the War she scrabbled dangerously for it in the rubble of bomb-shattered Canterbury and, mangled though it was, soon rode it again. Margaret Babbington was not easily defeated.

Her father had been the Vicar of Tenterden and when her mother died early, it was Margaret who took over her multifarious parish duties. In her maturity she was appointed as Honorary Steward and Treasurer of the Friends of Canterbury Cathedral by Dean Bell to carry on the work he had started in the 20's.

Her fervent aim was not merely the workaday maintenance of the Cathedral but also its rich embellishment. To this end she worked tirelessly to raise money - and almost as tirelessly to spend it. Nothing was too good for the Cathedral, or for the Festival of Friends she helped to organise. She imported leading conductors and talented soloists as well as famous poets and playwrights to add lustre to it: T. S. Eliot's 'Murder in the Cathedral', Dorothy Sayers' 'Zeal of Thy House', Laurie Lee's 'Peasant Priest' . . . As a result the Friends had occasionally to pay out (blessedly?) rather more than they received. The Cathedral Chapter was not amused!

But such amounts were a comparative bagatelle for she undertook gruelling tours in America to give as many as 50 lectures! The last, made when she was nearly 80, resulted in a handsome £9,000 in the kitty.

During 1953 she was an all too regular visitor to the Kent and Canterbury Hospital. Slowly, painfully, she was being crippled by arthritis. There was no more cycling but she still worked early and late at her desk. And as she prepared optimistically for one last lecture tour, it was at her desk, and with a smile on her lips, that she died.

She worked also for the Kent County Nursing Association. And, during the War, for the W.V.S. Despite constant Alarms, wailing like banshees, she never willingly left her post.

In all, she worked for nearly 30 years for 'her' Cathedral and, with her team, raised £100,000 to beautify it. Her book, 'The Romance of Canterbury Cathedral' is short and simple but rich in 'word pictures' of the memorable events which took place in it over the centuries. They range from its horrendous destruction by fire in 1011 to the vainglorious presentation by Henry VIII of a kneeling silver figure of himself 'to be set as nigh to the shrine of St Thomas as well may be'.

She also lectured brilliantly on the rich heraldry of the Cloisters - and it was in the Cloister Garth that her ashes were interred. A plaque nearby; another in the South aisle of the Cathedral itself; many of the building's embellishments; and Archbishop Cosmo Lang's words: '. . . that most active and enthusiastic of the Friends' are her memorial.

BACCELLI, Giannetta

Kept Woman . . .

A CHARMING little something that John Sackville, 3rd Duke of Dorset, brought back with him as a souvenir from his stay in Paris as Ambassador. A stay which ended abruptly in 1789! A dancer, she originated from Italy and happily joined the Duke's growing list of battle honours - amongst whom it was whispered, whispered very quietly indeed, had been Marie Antoinette herself!

Giannetta was fittingly accommodated in a tower next to the splendid archway which had been built at Knole by Archbishop Bourchier: a case of courtesan and Canterbury. Today it is known as Shelley's Tower. Not a reference to the equally spirited and passionate English poet but simply because in those days even Ducal servants couldn't watch television ads for lush Italian ice-cream! Had they been able to, Giannetta Baccelli's name would have rolled from their tongues as mellifluously as Gino Gianelli or Romano Ruggiero. As it was, Shelley was the best they could manage.

Should you wish to meet this nubile Italian beauty in person then pause at the bottom of Knole's Great Staircase with its newel-posts crowned by arrogant Sackville leopards. There, at its foot, in cool marmoreal nudity, the Italian ballerina lies - with some modesty - across plump cushions.

Some 200 years ago she was hustled, in no small indignity, to the dusty, deserted attics. The Duke had, rather belatedly, turned over a new leaf and married Arabella Cope, a woman with dignity, character - and very considerable expectations.

BENNETT, Joseph

Donkey impresario . . .

HE was known as a man of 'notoriety and eccentricity' - but one with a good nose for business. He was the first to spot donkey potential at England's seaside resorts. Early in the 19th century he set up an Asinarium or Donkey Stud. Its long-eared occupants, together with some outcast ponies, 'numbered upwards of three score'.

Banners fluttering in the sea breeze, drums beating, trumpets blaring, drivers cracking their whips in unison, and Bennett at their head, they made a stirring spectacle as they headed for the beach.

Here, for 1/- (5p) an hour, and a tip for the boy who led them, they plodded patiently up and down the beach. Generally, it was a case of 'ladies up'. Though - 'purely for the sake of fun and frolic' - their more dignified gentlemen friends could be persuaded, after much pretty feminine pouting and pleading, to accompany them.

BLOUNT, Richard (1565-1638)

Pertinacious Priest . . .

THERE was no hint in Blount's youth that he would put his staunchly Protestant parents to shame when he left their Leicestershire home at Osbaston, for Oxford. They had counted without Father Robert Parsons, a Jesuit 'sleeper' who so subtly indoctrinated Blount that Protestant turned Catholic and fled with him to Spain.

There he and others were smuggled into the presence of a Spanish Admiral at Cadiz. And by him they were given the tattered clothes of English sailors captured when Essex's expedition had sunk ships destined for the Armada. Equally important, they were given detailed and graphic information on how the battle had gone.

So, suitably hollow-eyed, and with beards and hair unkempt from their 'privations' in Spanish prisons, they made their way back to England. Back also to searching interrogation by the Lord High Admiral of the Fleet, Howard of Effingham himself. So well had they been briefed that, unsuspected, they were sent on their way - to further the cause of Elizabeth's enemy, Spain, and the Catholic Church. By word and by whisper, Secretary Burghley, whom little escaped, got a whiff of the subterfuge - but it was too late. The tracks were cold.

Had they been warmer, doubtless Elizabeth's pursuivants, her Warrant Officers, would have followed them to William Darell at moated and machicolated Scotney Castle (near Lamberhurst). Darell was a fervent Romanist who had written numerous religious tracts ranging from 'Conduct of a Virtuous and Happy Life' (which included 'A Word to the Ladies') to 'The Vanity of Human Respects'. More importantly, when repairing the rambling castle he had had the foresight to make several priest-holes deep in the thick walls. Ideal for sheltering wanted men such as Richard Blount. So, for eight years he lived there - if such a dank, dark life under constant fear of betrayal can be called living. Like a spider, he sat in the middle of his web of espionage and recruitment, working and organising through innumerable letters and trusted couriers. Like this he lived until Christmas week in 1598 when scraps of rumour brought the pursuivants hurrying to Scotney to search, hammer and probe - unsuccessfully.

That is until, to her horror, Darrell's wife saw the end of Blount's girdle protruding from a secret door. Her desperately whispered, 'Pull it in! For God's sake, pull it in!' brought them running at the double. Despite all her autocratic airs and her excuses their suspicions were aroused. Still more fiercely the search was renewed until storm and darkness drove them to call it a day.

The 'rats' had to bolt . . . There was nothing else for it. Blount's colleague, Father Bray, chose his moment and, silent as a wraith, tiptoed out. Then, without hesitation, ran to the searchers, laughing and drinking in the Great Hall, bellowing 'Fire! Fire! To the stables! Save your horses! Save your horses' and hurried the unquestioning pursuivants through a maze of shadowy corridors towards the distant outbuilding - before, in the noisy panic, he slipped away into the darkess. Blount waited only to hear the hue and cry, then unhesitatingly clambered over the moat wall, plunged into its icy waters, and swam to safety.

Or to be more exact, 'to the house of a lady of rank'. There still planning, sill scheming, Blount stayed for the rest of his life. For 18 years none of the servants ever saw him. And when he himself undertook a mission he went by night - and returned by night. Such were the sacrifices willingly made for the Catholic Faith by Richard Blount, the first Jesuit Provincial Superior of England.

BLUE, Little Bit of

A Sally Gunnell of her Day . . .

SADLY, the author can offer the merest glimpse of this virtually anonymous but intriguing young lady.

It all began and, as far as he can trace, finished at a match played in 1744 between Eleven Men of Kent and Eleven Gentlemen of the Borough of Southwark. It was a double-bill affair which would have made the razamataz of American Football and even Erica Roe's much acclaimed Twickenham 'streak' seem like a Sunday School outing.

The players had subscribed, not over generously perhaps, for a 'Holland smock value one guinea' which was to be run for by 'two jolly wenches'. It was firmly stipulated that 'they are to run only in their drawers' and not unnaturally prophesied that 'an excellent sport is expected'.

Obviously aware of the event's drawing power, the promoters had wisely arranged that 'Captain Vinegar with a great many of his bruisers and bulldogs will attend to make a ring that no civil spectators will be incommoded by the rabble'.

Unfortunately time has drawn a tantalisingly discreet veil over the scene. It is not known whether 'The Little Bit of Blue' (the handsome Broom Girl) or 'Black Bess of the Mint' was the first to swing into the straight and generously breast the tape doubtless to the derisory wolf whistles of that day.

CAESAR, Julius (100 BC - 44 BC)

Veni, Vidi, Vici . . .

PERFECTLY true (and couldn't have been put more succinctly) but what sort of man was this bald-headed womanizing general bent on raping what was to become Kent? Like many another foreigner intent on exploring England he reconnoitred until bad weather forced a retreat. Then, intrigued, came again for a longer stay.

In early youth he was priest, to Jupiter; poet, whose delicate touch disappeared in the crisply muscular style of his self-glorifying 'De Bello Gallico' (which was to give such grief to generations of bemused English schoolboys); and shrewd jurist whose indictment of profligate Publius Dolabella won him acclaim from the people of Rome.

Caesar took part in crushing the rising of the slaves under Spartacus which ended in 6,000 of these unfortunates being crucified along the

Appian Way. Captured by pirates, he harangued them mercilessly for setting his ransom at so low, so demeaning a figure. And when released, crucified the lot!

As a general he was a gambler; but a gambler who led his men into the hottest part of the battle. A strict disciplinarian too but with a grin he would maintain of his troops, 'They fight as well stinking of perfume.' And was himself an ardent womanizer. So much so that the awards of oak wreath, and laurels meant more to him as means of concealing his steadily increasing baldness than as honorific awards.

'Home we bring our bald whoremonger;
Romans, lock your wives away
All the bags of gold you lent him
Went his Gallic tarts to pay.'

After his unprecedented bridging of the turbulent Rhine - and a cold-blooded massacre - he cast around for greater glory: crossing the Channel (though jealous Pompey scathingly dismissed it as 'no more than a mudflat'); over-running another country; establishing lucrative trade . . .

At the end of the fighting season he planned his reconaissance of the 'strange land at the extremities of the earth' - and embarked his favourite Legions into 80 transports and war-galleys. On 25 August 55 BC Caesar and his armada arrived off Dover. There, cliff-tops bristling with warlike Britons sent him prudently further north to Deal: to its steeply sloping beaches and unaccustomed swirling tides.

In the latter, his heavily armoured legionaries might have retreated before the javelins and chariots of the Cantii . . . Only the rallying cry of the 10th Legion's standard-bearer calling upon their gods and upon their courage sent them surging forward again. Nature, however, as well as the Cantii, was against him. A sudden vicious storm forced the vessels belatedly bringing his cavalry to turn about and head back to Boulogne. And it sent his badly moored ships crashing and splintering one into another. Cohorts turned shipwrights: spear was changed for adze. But with winter closing in there was nothing for it but that word hardly known to Caesar, 'Retreat'. Retreat with no booty and little real knowledge of Britain. Superbly disciplined, backs to the sea, the Roman Legions carried out their orderly Dunkirk. For such failure the Senate honoured him with 20 days of feasting!

Within a year brash Caesar was preparing, not for another reconaissance but for all-out invasion - and conquest. Backed by the power and might of the Roman Empire, no fewer than 800 ships assembled off Boulogne. It was an armada not to be equalled in size for 2,000 years. Many of the vessels had been built by merchants, would-be profiteers eager for trade or booty: corn and iron, pearls and tin, slaves . . . Though the latter may well have become something of a drug on the market for in the Forum, Cicero had been heard to say, 'Do not buy British slaves; they are totally deficient in all civilised attainments'.

This time the uncultured but now wiser Britons did not sweep down in wild fury on the invaders. So, after three days, with base camp established, Caesar felt it safe to march 16 miles by night over the Downs to seize the crossing at Tonford (just outside Canterbury) of the Great Stour. And to storm that 'well-fortified post of great strength' Bigbury Camp. That was achieved only after close-ranked legionaries, with shields raised high and flat over their bent backs, had, like giant armadillos, crashed through their defences.

After yet another unfriendly storm had wrought havoc among his fleet, Caesar pushed on westwards from the Kent coast . . . to the Thames. It was guerilla warfare for the woad-painted Britons avoided pitched battle, in which Caesar could crushingly deploy the full weight of his five legions, as determinedly as Caesar sought it. Instead, their horsemen and chariots - 4,000 of them, wrote Caesar, but then he was prone to self-enhancing exaggeration - swept down on his troops from out of the surrounding forests, then as swiftly disappeared into them, tantalising and as insubstantial as ghosts.

But on the stake-lined banks of the Thames the Britons did at last stand firm. Even at this fording-point, the Thames was broad, if not as broad as the Rhine. So Caesar played his trump card, his psychological ace . . . a single elephant! Trumpeting wildly, it swayed down into the river and from the howdah on its back, javelins, spears, stones and arrows brought death to the shocked Britons. Panic-stricken they wavered and fled.

Back at base, Cassivellaunus had magically welded four squabbling tribes into one powerful armed force. They launched a last mass attack. Only to be routed by Roman discipline. Caesar, haunted now by difficulties of provisioning his troops; the imminent approach of winter; and festering rebellion in Gaul, seized his chance. Poker-faced, he dictated swingeing terms for peace. Submission to Rome; hostages to be handed over; and annual tribute to be paid. Then, savagely speeded on his way by yet another storm, he turned his back on Kent and England.

Nearly 100 years were to pass before, in 43 AD, under the command of Claudius, Romans returned to subjugate all but the very north of Britain. Nevertheless it was Caesar who had laid the first foundations of the new Romano-British way of life that was to endure for 400 years. Today they are still evident in Kent at Richborough and Lullingstone, Dover and Canterbury.

CAUSEY, Belle

Governess of the Wells . . .

EVEN before Beau Nash took over as Master of Ceremonies at The Wells, it was she who collected for balls and banquets, and for charity. 'A fine, but very large woman' she did it by sheer bulk and by choosing her time shrewdly.

As visitors poured out of the Church of King Charles the Martyr, already softened up by the Vicar's call to that greatest of the Three Virtues, Charity, she stood impassable in front of the door. Her spotless apron, held wide open and in front of her, was silently demanding. It was a virtue she herself practised as she gave generously to the poor.

Before taking over The Wells, her scene had been The Ring in Hyde Park. Here her nubile nymphs sold oranges nearly as ripe as themselves; and acted discreetly as carriers of more dangerous fruit: billet-doux from simpering dandy or rake to eager virgins or wealthy widows. And like today's 'Saturday Rendezvous' in 'The Times' was always ready 'to promote friendship between persons of the highest rank'.

Tunbridge Wells owed her much.

CHURCHILL, Sir Winston Leonard Spencer (1874-1965)

Man of Action; Man of Vision . . .

BORN at Blenheim Palace: a descendant of the first great Duke of Marlborough, via his father, Sir Randolph Churchill, Chancellor of the Exchequer (1856) and Jenny Jerome, American society beauty. Honoured in London as first among equals. Globe-trotter in peace and war. Author and orator. Such in brief was the man whom Labour's Clement Atlee described as 'the greatest Englishman of our time'.

Winston passed through Harrow with scarcely a ripple, but it caused a family stir when, as a young man, he was knocked down by a New York taxi which left him with a deep cleft, running down his forehead, that was to add to, rather than detract from, his bulldog look.

It was at Sandhurst that he made his mark . . . and emerged as an officer of the 4th Hussars. As such he engaged in bitter hand to hand fighting at Omdurman in the Sudan with the fanatical Dervishes, murderers of General 'Chinese' Gordon; with the Boers too, as war correspondent from whose capture he adroitly escaped with a vastly under-priced reward of £25 on his head.

He turned from the war of weapons to the war of words. In politics he was something of a maverick, changing his Parliamentary coat from blue to yellow - and back to blue. His early days in the Commons, from 1900, were a 'study in failure'. For all that, when War broke out in 1914, he was at the Admiralty, to become the 'father of naval aviation'. But in 1915 he was made a scapegoat for the disastrous, year-long Dardanelles campaign he had over-optimistically planned to knock out a staggering Turkey and to relieve a hard-pressed Russia. Resigning, he plunged into the thick of the war on the Western Front with his battalion of the Royal Scots Fusiliers.

In 1917, Lloyd George, recognising his abilities, offered him the post of Minister of Munitions. 'Can a bloody duck swim?' he asked before eagerly taking up this key position. His first action, in which he was helped by his wife, Clemmie, was the seemingly mundane introduction of canteens for his tens of thousands of workers. It was a shrewd move which helped him to pioneer and speed up the production of his brain-children, the lumbering tanks which eventually did much to end the hideous slaughter of frontal infantry attacks.

For a decade he showed his versatility in the government of Stanley Baldwin of whom he was to remark, 'He occasionally stumbled over the truth, hastily picked himself up - and carried on as if nothing had happened'. He was in turn Secretary for War, Air, and the Colonies until finally he became Chancellor of the Exchequer, and brought England back onto the Gold Standard. At the next General Election, however, he was not re-elected. And in his own words he found himself 'without any office; without a seat; without a Party - and without an appendix.' Never a man to waste time, he followed his four-volume 'The World Crises' (1923-1929) with another book of similar outstanding length on his distinguished soldier-ancestor, the Duke of Marlborough (1933-1938).

* * * * *

In 1922, with an unexpected legacy, he had bought 'Chartwell', perched high on the Kentish Greensand Hills, near Westerham. Bought it, not for the Victorian ivy-clad house, but for the view across the rolling Kentish Weald. It was one of which he never tired during his lifetime.

Its open-raftered study ('like some miniature Westminster Hall') was where, in the haze of Havana cigars and under the eyes of his porcelain heroes, Napoleon and Nelson, he worked tirelessly far into the night. Distinguished visitors, whose signed photos still line one staircase, were frequent. They ranged from Field-Marshal Montgomery ('unbeatable in defeat; unbearable in victory') to Aircraftsman Shaw, one-time Lawrence of Arabia, who having arrived on his thunderous motorbike 'Boanerges', would often dine in his hard-earned flowing white robes of an Arabian prince.

Churchill's interests were manifold. He landscaped the garden; promoted the lower pool to islanded lake; installed in the garden a swimming pool with 'boilers big enough to heat the Ritz' tucked out of sight beneath it. A Union card-holder, he slipped easily from the bricklayer's trowel, used to build a tall - and expensive - wall which included a 'real house' for his young daughter, to the artist's brush. With the latter, he joyously followed the advice of Sir John Lavery's wife: 'Wallop on the blue and white . . .' and then fell upon the cowering canvas with almost berserk fury to powerful effect.

He preferred bezique to croquet which his wife played with Monty, a master strategist at Alamein but a tyro on the Chartwell lawn. In his zip-up siren suit and his vast Mexican sombrero, Churchill would sit and commune with his golden orfe in its pool; admire his Australian black swans on the lake; and even walk with a deeply attached but malodorous sheep. And he admitted, 'I take more out of alcohol than alcohol takes out of me'.

* * * * *

Not that all was pleasure in his 1930's wilderness years out of office. To attacks on his canvases he added ceaseless war on the supine Government which eventually cringed before Hitler at Munich. There, Neville Chamberlain misguidedly trusted the latter's tongue-in-cheek agreement to renounce war. But for all the Prime Minister's triumphantly waved 'scrap of paper', Churchill the more vehemently urged re-armament. When an inefficient Chamberlain was forced to resign shortly after he had declared War, it was, of course, Churchill who determinedly seized the reins of office in a Coalition government.

All he could offer a stunned people was 'Blood, sweat and tears', and bulldog defiance of the all-conquering Hitler. 'We will fight on the beaches . . . we shall never surrender.' The story of his inspirational oratory and leadership that brought Britain, alone, and once virtually out on the ropes, to victory is too well known to need recounting here.

Honoured by King and country alike, he was, in 1945, astonishingly rejected by an ungrateful electorate with its mind now firmly fixed on present work rather than on past war. He was succeeded by his wartime Deputy, Clement Atlee, of whom he had once said: 'A modest man with much to be modest about: a sheep in sheep's clothing.' Just as Churchill had urged rearmament pre-War, now he sounded the danger of the newly roused giant, Russia, which had tasted blood . . . For nearly 50 years the world was to echo with the bleak phrase that he had coined: 'The Iron Curtain'. His History of the Second World War was published in 1948.

In 1951, now 77, he bounced back into office. But by then the tireless energy which had driven him through 18-hour war-days and over 150,000 miles of travel by land, sea and air, had diminished. At 80, he resigned - reluctantly. But he could still find the mental resources to write the four-volume 'A History of the English-speaking People' (1956-58).

It was an Augustan masterpiece, written with the care for style that had led him, tongue in cheek, furiously to denounce slipshod Whitehall memoranda. 'This is the sort of English up with which I will not put.' And which had caused him to tell his secretaries never to write that 'Mr Churchill was most gratified' because no one except himself could possibly know whether such was the case'.

Persuaded, with some difficulty, not to contest one last election when he was 90, he retired, sadly, from the Commons: a Commons which he had graced and galvanized for 65 years. Shortly after, his work done, he died.

Fittingly, he was given a State funeral, a rare honour seldom granted to a commoner. When his body was taken on the first stage of his carefully planned last journey to the little village of Blaidon, near Blenheim, even the Port of London cranes bowed spontaneously in a last tribute.

❧

COOPER, Thomas Sydney (1803-1902)

Animal artist supreme . . .

'**B**LINDLY infatuated', Thomas's father deserted his five children when Thomas was just five. His mother, Sara, now utterly destitute except for her own meagre earnings, had little time to supervise the youngster. Fortunately Canterbury Cathedral's majesty and bulk captured his imagination; fired a youthful ambition to become a painter. By the time he was nine he was drawing skilfully on his school slate.

Such formal teaching as he did receive was at the National School, near St Dunstan's level-crossing. His headmaster, a Mr Abram, he remembered as in a constant haze of snuff from which he emerged only occasionally to gaze at his 50-strong class as if they were invisible spirits. The usher, Mr Mazella, who, despite his name was an English sadist to the core, he had good cause to remember better. For he kept their noses in their books by pleasurably cutting timidly proferred knuckles with piece of slate.

Thomas's art education was just as sketchy - but happier. He learnt colour mixing from a kindly doctor; perspective from a scenery painter; smoothness of texture from a coach builder; and more advanced drawing in general from a Mr Martyn, 'the finest teacher in Kent'. It was Cooper's ability to teach the younger boys which was used in lieu of money to pay his fees.

Seeking wider fields and using his skill as a portraitist he sought his fortune across the Channel, in Brussels. There he was inspired by the

21

sunlit landscapes of the 17th century Dutch Master, Cuyp; and was taken into the studio of Eugene Verboeckhoven, a master painter of animals. Thomas Cooper's lifelong inflexible style was being formed.

Patronage too came early. When he was nine! Busily drawing, he asked a benevolent looking old gentleman crossing the Precincts if he could spare the time to sharpen his pencils. This he - the Most Reverend Charles Manners-Sutton, Archbishop of Canterbury - did without demur. Admired his drawing; promised him 5/- for the completed work of art; and eventually paid him, not 5/- but £5 for the finished picture.

This was the first of Cooper's hundreds of prints and paintings. The former were of picturesque 19th century Canterbury; the latter of its gentle countryside, and of cattle of every description: heavily fleeced sheep, sleek cows and their calves; magnificent bulls; alert deer; a Scots collie that would dry off his master's rain-sodden plaid by holding it up in front of the fire; and even a dejected donkey.

His most prestigious painting was of Buffie - Guernsey's gift to Queen Victoria and Prince Albert. This gentle beast he painted at Osborne by Command before discerning Royal eyes. His largest? 259 cms x 223 cms, three-quarters life size: 'Separated but not Divorced' is of Charley, a handsome shorthorn bull with his harem in the background. Unfortunately he had to spend nearly as much time repainting the head, of which his wife did not approve, as he had on the whole picture. His most unusual? 'The Half-past One O'clock Charge at Waterloo' in which there were no fewer than 800 figures of men and horses in fierce action.

His most expensive? 'Monarch of the Meadows', so called after the success of Landseer's 'Monarch of the Glen'. It was exhibited at the Royal Academy, tagged at £2,500 at a time when an agricultural labourer toiled in all weathers for 12/6d a week. A Mr Allcroft offered 2,000 guineas but was so delighted with the picture once it was in his home that he gladly paid the original £2,500.

Such sales and exhibitions at the Royal Academy for over 60 years made him a very rich man. A generous one too: bread and coal for the very poor of *his* City of Canterbury; extra tea, bread and meat for his harvesters. Much more generous were his gifts of a Civic Theatre and a College of Art. When the old theatre in Orange Street ground to decrepit halt, it was Thomas, at a personal cost of over £5,000, who built a concert hall and theatre in Guildhall Street where today Debenhams lords it. He built it out of civic pride, a love of Shakespeare, and perhaps because of Lord Bessborough's hint, 'No theatre - no Old Stagers (dramatic performances) - no Cricket Week'. Quite, quite unthinkable. Within a year of its opening, one of Cooper's legion of friends, Charles Dickens, gave a rivetting dramatic reading of 'David Copperfield' - it was one of the many that hastened the latter's death.

Cooper bought 64 St Peter's Street, his birthplace, as a tribute to his hardworking mother. With neighbouring buildings added, he turned it into a College of Art. Here, youngsters were to find learning much easier than he had done - and at ld per session much cheaper too. He taxed his own health to the limit by, apart from his own ceaseless studio work, teaching three times a week a group of up to 50. Before the end of the session in which he had enthusiastically dovetailed explanation and demonstration, he would have criticised and amended the work of every class member!

Money was spent too on over 400 acres of property in the district. On a hop field at Harbledown he built his own large, self-designed house, Vernon Holme (now a Preparatory School). It was named after his first real patron who had made his own fortune first by selling horses to the Army during the Napoleonic Wars, and then by knowledgeably investing it in artists and their pictures.

Two of Cooper's most interesting purchases were mills that he generously took off the hands of his second wife's parents when milling was in decline. Nevertheless he modernised them so that between them they could provide 600 sacks a week. Of white weatherboard they loomed over the City almost as majestically as the Cathedral.

Abbot's Mill had been designed, in 1792, by John Smeaton of Eddystone Lighthouse fame as a successor to mills dated back to King Stephen and Henry II. Dean's Mill (later Hooker's) dated back nearly as far, to the times of Richard the Lionheart. Both were destroyed in horrific conflagrations; the former in 1933, burning for seven days and nights; the latter in 1954.

In 1901, Cooper was told that he was to be decorated with the Royal Victorian Order by King Edward himself if he could make it to Marlborough House. Although nearly 98, nothing would deter him from the exhausting journey. And only six months later, after ten bronchial attacks in nine years, Cooper was laid to rest in St Martin's Church graveyard, aged 98 years, 4 months and 12 days.

COURTENAY, Sir William (c. 1796-1838)

Madman . . .

COUNT Moses Rothschild was the name on the register of the Rose Inn (1832). And when such a name was accompanied by a man of striking appearance, obviously a foreigner, in flamboyant clothes, Canterbury tongues wagged. Wagged still more when lusty rumour had it that this open-handed Milord received a barrelful of sovereigns every fortnight.

Shock piled on shock. Within days the Count then claimed to be not Rothschild but Sir William Honeywood Courtenay, a Knight of Malta. Unhesitatingly he nominated himself as an election candidate against two local gentlemen. Even on such short acquaintance he polled heavily - but unavailingly.

But then with promises of the abolition of both the hated tithes and the taxation of shopkeepers, it was hardly surprising. Besides, he put his policies across with such theatrical panache: speaking from balconies from which he threw down coins to the mob below; on horseback; even on a pyramid of other men's shoulders!

In Oriental costume and with a scimitar hung from his neck he paraded the streets accompanied by fifes and drums - and challenged four local gentlemen to duels to the death. Almost overnight, however, he suddenly became King of Jerusalem, Prince of Arabia, King of the Gypsies! 'I worship Truth as my God' was his new cry. But he spoilt the Christian illusion when he obviously perjured himself when, seeking popularity, he supported nefarious Kent smugglers. He was sentenced to seven years transportation - finally reduced however to confinement at Barming Asylum, near Maidstone.

Within four years he was free. This was largely due to the misguided efforts of Mr Toole, MP for Truro. For that is where poor John Nichols Thom (alias Sir William Courtenay) had been born of a publican father and a mother who herself had become insane. J. W. Banks of the 'British Lion' may have written: 'His moral character exceeded that of anyone I ever knew' but still 'of unsound mind' had been the Asylum's opinion even though it went unheeded on his release.

Within weeks, deluded perhaps by his own patriarchal beard and a chance heard remark, Moses became Messiah, complete with stigmata and the power to work miracles! At least he was a Messiah with a worthy cause: a better life for ill-paid farm labourers who, when out of work, could expect no Poor Law relief, only the cold charity of the Union Workhouse. He offered them the unobtainable carrot of 50 acres of their own land; and the stick of 'If you desert me, I will follow you to the further part of Hell, and invoke fire and brimstone on you from Heaven'.

When, in 1838, they rallied to his banner, a loaf of bread on a pole, prosperous Farmer Curling hastily called out Constable Mears only for him to be ruthlessly shot by the not-so-peaceful Messiah. The Vicar of Hernhill and four J.P.s fled from a similarly hostile reception.

Now there was nothing for it but the 45th Militia. Peaceful Bossenden Wood, near Dunkirk, became a battlefield. Lt Bennett leading the advance and Special Constable Catt both died. Shot by Thom's pistols. So too did desperate and deluded farm labourers, armed only with scythes and oak cudgels . . . Eight of them from musket shot and bayonet wounds.

Courtenay too was killed. Hundreds flocked to the Red Lion at Hernhill to see his shattered body. His bloodstained shift was ripped to pieces by his disciples to obtain a relic of the 'martyr'. To frustrate grave robbers he was buried secretly, at night, in an unmarked grave of which there is no trace today.

In reprisal, the rebels sadly reaped death and transportation from a seed they themselves had not sown. Yet all was not entirely in vain for an official enquiry was held into 'The State of the Peasantry in the County of Kent'.

CULMER, Richard (Died 1662)

Iconoclast . . .

'BLUE DICK' (conventional black suits would have much better matched his mean spirit but he always dressed in blue) was born at Broadstairs. By a quirk of fate however he was educated at King's School, Canterbury in the shadow of the magnificent Cathedral he was to violate At Magdalen, Oxford, he was remembered for his qualities as a trencherman with an insatiable appetite for boiled buttered beans rather than as an academic.

His first curacy, in 1630, was a shortlived one at Goodnestone. Shortlived because he refused to read to his congregation from the Book of Sport: an official edict which urged, rather than condemned, Sunday games. Suspended, 'this turbulent unquiet man' recklessly tried to bribe a strongly disapproving Archbishop Laud into giving him the living at Chartham.

Despite this, or was it because of it, in 1643 he was nominated with others 'to demolish and destroy Idolatrous Monuments in Canterbury Cathedral'. It was a task he performed with evil relish. Drunken soldiery had already used the figure of Christ set in a niche high up on the Christ Church Gateway for target practice. And, on his urging, later lassooed it, and dragged it, shattered, to the ground. Swiftly Culmer did his piece: 'Many idolls of stone were smashed; Christ and His Apostles above the Quire entrance were hewn down; the richly embroidered Glory Altar Cloth was destroyed by Flame and Fire' . . .

And to climax this orgy of destruction, pike in hand, he climbed the 56 rung City ladder, 'so high none dared follow', to shatter Edward IV's towering Royal Window in the north-west transept. He revelled in thus 'rattling down proud Becket's glassy bones - in all his Pontificalibus'; and 'Seven several appearances of the Virgin Mary'.

Appalled, worshippers looked on helplessly, able only to pray - that he might break his neck. One went even further, narrowly missing him 'with a good thumping stone' when Culmer vaingloriously boasted 'I am doing the Lord's work'.

In his spleen, Culmer also published scurrilous tales of Laud. But in 'Antidotum Culmerianon' the Archbishop gave as good as he got: 'His inke is mixte of vinegar and kennel water.'

For his success in destroying every image of Christ (but never of the Devil) that he could find, Parliament appointed this Puritan fanatic as one of the cathedral's usually distinguished Six Preachers. Worse still, the scholar Meric Casaubon was ejected from his living at Minster to make way for him. There, Culmer seeking 'to read himself in' smashed his way into the church when he found it locked and barred by his parishioners whom he had already infuriated - and who now soundly beat him for his pains. Revenge however was his. He tore down the crucifixes on the spire which his flock venerated - and thereafter rode all attacks on himself by word or blow until he was finally ousted at the Restoration.

CUSHING, Peter (1913-1995)

A horror . . . !

A VERY gentle man too who nursed a much loved wife through her last illness. Yet, in appearance, cold, cadaverous, with hair fast receding from his temples above a gaunt face . . . This, and a helping hand from the make-up girl, type-cast him in 'Frankenstein and the Monster', 'Brides of Dracula', 'Hell Masks of Death', 'Flesh and Fiends' . . . He sent cold shivers of delight down the backs of millions of cinema and television addicts. And became the star of the Hammer House of Horror.

Fortunately he was not eternally typecast as a graveyard ghoul. After a trip to America, when his career seemed to be going nowhere, he was to be seen, or perhaps not seen, as 'The Man in the Iron Mask'. He was to have his meditative moments too in 'Hamlet' as well as in 'Dr Who and the Daleks'. His natural urbanity and the voice, trained at the Guildhall School of Drama, served him well as Sherlock Holmes.

1955 saw him Television Actor of the Year when he played the hapless Winston Smith in George Orwell's '1984' - with its modern sadism more horrifying than Dracula and Frankenstein rolled into one. 'Pipe Man of the Year' too!

For many years he lived in Whitstable near Sea Wall. And anyone foolish enough to be about at that hour would have seen him emerge quietly from his house at 5.30 am. Walk a brisk 4 miles. Plunge into a chilly ('the chillier the more invigorating') North Sea. Back home to an invariable breakfast of cornflakes (a modeller himself, he eagerly collected the free models they offered). And at lunch, porridge! A fitness fanatic who in his quieter moments painted landscapes and read avidly. His hobby, collecting cigarette cards, he maintained saved his sanity when, in 1971, his much loved wife Helen died. 'They are little mines of information and for a few minutes at least I could forget my sorrow. Without them - and my books - I should have gone mad.'

He also delighted in model figures. For them he built a working theatre which boasted ten scenes, all from different plays and different periods. His cast was equally impressive: no fewer than 128 actors and actresses bestrode his stage. Over half of them had been specially commissioned for master modeller, Frederic Ping.

A record breaker with 90 films in 50 years!

DADD, Richard (1817-1886)

Pursued by the Devil . . .

SURPRISINGLY perhaps Dadd and Van Gogh did have something in common. In style the former's delicate and imaginative masterpiece 'The Fairy Feller's Master Stroke' had little of Van Gogh's landscapes and their dazzling colour. No, the similarity lay, not in their styles of painting but in the sun - the sun that drove both to madness.

Richard was born in Brompton, Chatham where his father, Robert, a chemist and 'a man of rectitude and moral certainty' owned The Golden Mortar. Had he only been less certain the horrible tragedy that followed might never have happened.

Young Dadd attended King's School, Rochester, an ancient church foundation of 1542. Its Headmaster was a Reverend with a reputation. His belief in the efficacy of the cane 'gradually flogged away every boy in the school' except for one - his own son. In 13 years his brutality reduced the school-roll steadily from 16 to just one.

When Richard was 19, his caring father moved to London so that his son's precocious artistic talent could be given richer growth at the Royal Academy School. There, with William Frith (later famous for 'Derby Day' and 'Margate Sands'), Augustus Egg, and three others, he helped to form 'The Clique'. It was a forum for art discussion - and the modest consumption of bread, cheese and beer.

Early in his career, Richard received a commission to illustrate 'The Ballad of Robin Goodfellow' from Carter Hall, editor of 'Art Union'. At the latter's house, 'The Rosary', which became better known as 'The Roguery' because of its owner's too shrewd business deals, he again consorted with other ambitious young artists. Despite having been brought up in Rochester amid Castle and Cathedral, Brompton's barracks, and Chatham's river and bustling dockyard, all so loved by Dickens, he opted 'to paint from the imagination'. Eventually however he experimented with every genre.

In 1842, fortune positively grinned on Dadd. Through the good offices of a fellow artist, he met the remarkable Sir Thomas Philips. The latter, a solicitor and Mayor of Newport, had, when defiantly reading the Riot Act to 7,000 seething Chartists, been accidentally shot - by one of his own supporters! Now, however, an overworked barrister in London, he needed a break, a holiday in the Middle East . . . and a companionable and able young artist who could record people and places. Thrilled, Richard leapt at this golden opportunity to travel widely and to further his skills and career all in a single throw.

However, in Venice he found the gondoliers 'the greatest scamps breathing'; Ancona was 'picturesque but full of knaves and cheats'; Corfu too was crowded with 'pompous ruffians'; Delphi was noisy with 'foul-mouthed washerwomen'; and Athens, 'all filth and ruin'.

Things improved considerably in Asia Minor though admittedly the fields were 'indifferently cultivated'; and even the jolly monks of St Anthony seemed to have a sinister aura. In Damascus he was pelted by a mob . . . On and on they swept in long, exhausting journeys with only the briefest of respites before they hurried on once more: a frenetic Cook's tour!

His frustrations grew. And always there was the sun. In his letters, he vividly described the sights - but with a growing underlying violence. Quarantine in Malta irked and depressed him . . . in Alexandria he had 'unaccountable impulses' . . . in Thebes he suffered indisposition and sunstroke . . . in Rome he had a strong inclination to attack the Pope . . . and in Paris he was showing open antagonism even towards his generous patron. Suddenly, haunted and hag-ridden, he hurried back to England.

Once there he made contact with his distraught father. Later, he arranged that they should holiday together for a few days at peaceful Cobham to talk over his problems. Doubtful, but determined to do his best for his son, Robert agreed. And one evening reluctantly undertook a late walk in Cobham Park. It was there that his hideously battered body was found next day!

Richard had fled to Dover. Then, in an open boat paid for with a wallet bulging with sovereigns and notes, on to Calais. When he boarded a train there for Paris his bloodstained suit ('a fall from a coach') had been replaced. En route, he chatted cheerfully enough with a fellow passenger - whilst inwardly debating whether this devil too must die. Only the portent of a cloudless sunset saved the stranger's life.

Next day, Dadd drove in a diligence with a Monsieur M. Again the voices urged him to kill . . . Racked with doubt, Dadd this time left it to Osiris, high in the evening sky above them. Its steady movement towards another star commanded 'Kill . . . Kill . . . Kill this devil'. Fortunately Monsieur M. was strong enough to overcome 'the envoy of God', the madman Richard Dadd. But only after he had suffered four bone-deep razor-cuts. Arrested, Richard spontaneously handed over all his money for the care of the victim!

Extradited to England, he was sent first to Bethlem; and then to recently built Broadmoor. Here the old regime of opiates and strait-jackets was replaced for him by colours, canvases and brushes. There, for over 40 years, Dadd, like a new man, painted 'with all the poetry of imagination but all the frenzy of insanity.' He painted people and scenes from his recent journeys conventionally enough.

But violence lurked in many of his long series of Hogarthian 'Passions': Hatred and Jealousy, Brutality and Drunkenness, Anger and Deceit. It was even more apparent in 'The Death of Richard II'; 'Crazy Jane'; and in portraits of his friends with their throats cut - drawn shortly after his admission to Bethlem and subsequently, wisely, 'lost'.

Far finer were his allegorical surrealist paintings. In the oddly named 'Fairy Feller's Master Stroke' and 'Oberon and Titania' his work was crowded with tiny, magical figures amid fantastic scenery where 'sparrows were giants; blades of grass, trees'. In 'Titania Sleeping' the Fairy Queen lies amid delicate nudes worthy of Etty's brush beneath an archway of tiny, grimacing hobgoblins. He painted in soft, clear colours, with the exactitude of a miniaturist.

Suffering from a disease of the lungs, he died in 1886, 'civil and well behaved but his mind still full of delusions'.

* * * * *

And in 1989, one of his paintings that had long hung unrecognised in an ordinary suburban house was taken to Sotheby's Antique Road Show - and later valued at £100,000.

'DISGUSTED' OF TUNBRIDGE WELLS

Swingeing scribes . . .

ANONYMOUS and vitriolic gentlemen who, at the turn of the century, erupted regularly in 'The Times' in Letters to the Editor. Probably an indignation (to coin a new collective noun) of disgruntled majors, ex-Indian Army, retired, who, returning to the Old Country found 'Gad, Sir, it's gone to the dogs!'. And trumpeted to that effect at every innovative modern trend. Their name became a by-word for deep-dyed, darkest blue Toryism.

DUNSTAN (c. 909-988)

Monk, Moralist, Musician . . .

AS a youth of great ability, the son of a West Saxon noble, and a courtier of King Athelstan, he had a flying start in life. But he was brought down to earth when his jealous peers first thrashed him, then ceremoniously threw him into a cesspit; and when he was curtly banished from court for 'practising unlawful acts'.

Courtier turned hermit at Glastonbury's ancient Abbey. It was left, however, to King Edmund fully to appreciate his abilities and, in 945, turn sensitive monk into reforming abbot. Into his own royal adviser as well. Under Dunstan's rule, the Abbey became a centre of learning without equal in the country.

On Edmund's death, again came the fall. His successor, Eadwig left his own coronation feast 'to dally with the girl, Elgiva' - and, regrettably, with her mother too! Only Dunstan among the Assembley had the courage to drive him from their warm bed. Not surprisingly, Eadwig, unforgivably and unforgettably humiliated, soon 'drove his mentor over the sea' - to Ghent.

Here he lived with Benedictine monks. And on his return to England he instilled into those monasteries still left standing by irreligious Vikings their Rule of 'Labour; Worship; and Prayer'; re-built those 'destroyed by the Heathen'; became, in 959, Archbishop of Canterbury; and replaced lax clergy with austere monks.

Not solely a religious reformer who practised rigid self-denial, Dunstan was also a phenomenally talented all-rounder: statesman and administrator, musician and harpist, who when he sang at the altar seemed 'to talk face to face with God'. Illuminater of glowing manuscrips, bell-founder and jeweller too. It was his jeweller's tongs which brought him to one of his not infrequent confrontations with the Devil. At Glastonbury, Old Nick has locked him out of his own Abbey - only for the angels to let him in. Now, in Kent, the Devil dared to tempt him with lewd thoughts. Enraged, Dunstan seized the Devil by the nose with his red-hot tongs . . . and threw him to the future site of Tunbridge Wells, to give its healing waters a sharp and sulphurous tang. Much more pacifically, legend had it that a dove fluttered down to settle on his shoulder during his enthronement as Archbishop in Canterbury Cathedral.

There he was to reign for 29 years before, quite casually, he mentioned to his horrified flock that he would shortly die: and set about deciding his burial place - near the High Altar. There, 24 years later, it was joined by that of his student, Alphege. Not that they were to remain there in peace. For cathedral rebuilding, especially after the grievous fires of 1070 and 1174, several times necessitated their removal to safer places.

Dunstan died just over a thousand years ago but his voice is still heard over Canterbury. (See Great Dunstan).

EDWARD, THE BLACK PRINCE (1330-1376)

'The Chief Flower of Chivalry of all the World' . . .

DUBBED DUKE OF CORNWALL at three; knighted at 15; titular commander of the right flank of the English army, over the Earls of Oxford and Warwick, at Crecy . . . made a pretty fair start for Edward, Prince of Wales.

Crecy was no mean blooding. The English were opposed by Philip Valois, 'Tyrant of the French'. His force of 60,000 men included 12,000 mounted knights and above it flew the scarlet and gold oriflamme, sacred symbol of a Holy War, and of the order 'No quarter'.

Only nightfall, the indiscipline of arrogant French knights, and the unflinching skill of the English archers (whose arrows fell 'so thick it seemed like snow') saved the day. Led by the blind John of Bohemia, rank upon rank of French knights, trumpets sounding, plumes and pennants waving, lances levelled, thundered down on the English lines.

Sheer weight of numbers seemed certain to break through the Black Prince's lines. So certain indeed that a fearful Godfrey de Harcourt hastened to implore the King for reinforcements only to receive the King's curt answer, 'Let the boy win his spurs.' He did just that. For on his return de Harcourt found the French in full retreat and the Prince leaning on his bloody sword amidst piles of the dead: 10,000 common soldiers and 1500 knights. As father and son walked the battlefield together, the former asked anxiously: 'What think you now of war as a sport?'

It was a victory worthily commemorated in the towering East Window of Gloucester Cathedral: 70' x 38', the largest in Europe. King and Prince surrounded by angels and archangels - and their loyal knights. Commemorated too by the foundation of the Order of the Garter: its badge, the Blue Garter inadvertently shed at a ball by Joan, the Fair Maid of Kent; its motto, 'Hon y soit qui mal y pense'. Commemorated too by the Prince's usurpation for his crest of the ostrich plumes of their gallant enemy, King John of Bohemia, at whose burial both Edward III and the Black Prince mourned. To military victory, in 1350, the Black Prince added naval victory. Off Dungeness his ships intercepted a marauding Spanish fleet. Though the English cobs and pinnaces were to the vessels of the latter 'as cottages to castles', no fewer than 17 ships were taken, thanks once again largely to the withering fire of the English archers which opened the way for boarding parties. As horses had been shot from beneath him at Crecy, so too his ship was sunk under him here. But it did nothing to prevent 'great revel at Pevensey Castle' that evening!

Six years later (1356) Le Prince Noir made his name immortal at Poitiers. A long marauding campaign had left him vast plunder and many prisoners for ransom but desperately short of wartime supplies. Left him too facing an army five times the size of his. 'Though we are but a small company let us not be abashed' he urged his exhausted troops. Tactically daring, he counter-attacked at the head of his knights when all seemed lost. And for all their gleaming armour and fluttering flags the great French host broke into headlong retreat. 'Like a lion in wrath he spared the lowly and took down the mighty'.

Took King John of France himself as prisoner. Fêted him that night and praised his valour with "rare and modest chivalry"; rode with him from Sandwich to Canterbury - he on a little black palfrey; the King on a handsome white charger; - and through the thronged and cheering streets of London.

It was however a chivalry that cooled when the French dragged their feet in finding their King's 300,000 crowns' ransom. And sadly it was a chivalry to be obliterated by a despairing animal fury at Limoges where he coldly watched the massacre of women and children as well as rebellious men. But Najera, in 1367, came first: here triumph turned into disaster. Chivalry (again) dictated that he supported the true Castillian king, Don Pedro, even though he was nicknamed 'The Cruel', against Don Enrico of Trastamora, the equally unsavoury, 'Bastard'.

After Edward had crossed the Pyrenees by the famous Ronscevalles Pass in biting wind and numbing cold; after months of sparring, 16,000 Spanish lay dead, a silent testimony to his brilliant flanking movement. But when Don Pedro showed more delight in slaying his prisoners than in paying Edward his due of a million crowns, the English army, now wracked by dysentry in the scorching heat of the Castillian plain, died in hundreds.

And it was that dysentry that in 1370 turned the once finely built man into a living skeleton. That forced him to be carried by arduous marches from Angouleme to Limoges, to wreak revenge on its citizens who in his absence had risen to slaughter the English garrison. Such French treachery and the spectre of Death before him tore chivalry to tatters. After a night attack, women and children as well as men were implacably put to the sword. Edward could be cruel as well as chivalrous; foul-mouthed as well as fair spoken. Too often historical distance can lend unjustified enchantment.

A final flurry foredoomed to failure saw Edward III's fleet routed not by French or Spanish ships but by a month long Channel storm. The king retired to his rapacious mistress's arms; the Prince to his castle. And in 1376, died there, mourned by the Good People and the Good Parliament which he had backed in their fight against new and heavy taxation. His last words (as transposed by Sir John Chandos, poet and herald) were:

'I recommend you to my son*
Who is yet both small and young,
And pray that as you served me
So from your heart you would serve him.'

Details of military carnage abroad may well make the reader wonder how such a man fits into a green and pleasant Kent. Edward was possibly educated by Prior Hathbrand and his Canterbury Cathedral monks. He dearly loved the Lady Undercroft chapel in the crypt and desired to be buried close to it; he built a chantry there in gratitude for Papal dispensation that allowed him to marry his cousin, Joan, the Fair Maid of Kent. And for six centuries he has lain, a cynosure of eyes, not in the crypt but in the very heart of the Cathedral next to the 'holy blissful martyr', Thomas à Becket.

There he still lies 'all armed in steel for battle' on the Purbeck marble tomb he himself designed. Hands joined in prayer; crested helm beneath his head; laughing bulldog at his feet. And above the 14th century canopy hang his achievements: helm, surcoat, shield, gauntlets and sword. Kent has no finer memorial.

* Richard II

GELDOF, Bob, K.B.E.

King of Pop . . .

A POP musician with sensitivity. Half a million people - real people, not mere statistics - had died in 1985 in Ethiopia and the Sudan of slow starvation.

Something had to be done. So Geldof did it. Arranged simultaneous concerts in London and Philadelphia to create the biggest rock jamboree the world had ever seen. At Wembley Stadium alone, 75,000 pop promenaders clapped and screamed their appreciation. The world watched on television - twice as many as had tuned in to see Man landing on the Moon.

And the world dug deep into its pocket. Enough to help but not to cure. It had a short term impact too on Geldof himself. Catastrophically, so he says. "It hit me personally as well as professionally. The public no longer thought of me as King of Rock - I was just 'Live Aid'."

Bob needed space and quiet. He found it at Davington Priory, near Faversham. Some 450 years before, the last Benedictine nuns - seeing the writing on the wall? - had left their home. Slowly, except for its church, the walls crumbled. But over the centuries they had been patched sufficiently for Geldof to find tranquility away from the racketing world of rock. Happily, at weekends, he shopped at Tesco's; helped put on the local annual Fête - and became just another citizen of Faversham.

GERMAIN, Lady Elizabeth ('Betty') (1680-1769)

Fifty years a widow . . .

EVEN though Lady Elizabeth was a daughter of the Earl of Berkeley, the viper-tongued Duchess of Marlborough did not hesitate to spit her malicious poison: 'She was very ugly; without a portion; and in her youth she had an unlucky accident with one of her father's servants. And she married an inn-keeper's son!'

Some inn-keeper! Some son! Her husband, many years her senior, (whom she had met at Bristol's Hot Wells) was Sir John Germain, the bastard, it was said, of a common Life Guard trooper and a lady of rank. As a soldier of fortune, with 'total lack of education, and morals so defective' that his affaire with the Duchess of Norfolk was the scandal of the Town, he became notorious.

Still more so, when the Duke denounced 'their lewd and lascivious conversations' - doubtless other things too - and, in the ways of the future 20th century, demanded £50,000 compensation to assuage his injured pride. The jury however felt his pride was not so delicate that it could not get by on a fiftieth of that amount.

Eventually Sir John inherited the vast estates of Drayton from his new wife, none other of course, than the Duchess. In due time he passed them on to Lady Betty together with the sincere wish that she should marry again: this time to a young and lusty man who would give her children. It was a wish she was never tempted to honour until, much older, but apparently little wiser, she nearly succumbed to the practised blandishments of Lord Sidney Beauclerc, a worthless fortune-hunter.

After 50 years of widowhood Lady Elizabeth did, however, pass on the Germain fortune - to Lord George Sackville, a son of the Duke and Duchess of Dorset. In gratitude, he changed his name to Germain but, later in life, did it little credit.

Though owner of Drayton, now crammed with pictures and fine china, Lady Betty preferred to live with her husband's distant kinsmen, the Dorsets, at Knole. There, in her two oak-panelled rooms, with a snug little four-poster bed, and her own prim portrait, are also reminders of the pot-pourri for which she was famous, and the innumerable letters that she wrote. Many of them were to her father's chaplain, the satirist Dean Swift, with whom, even as a youngster, she had delighted to engage in debate.

When she died, aged 89, it was justly said: 'She has outlived the irregularities of her youth and is much esteemed for her kindness and liberality'. Surely, a fitting epitaph.

***

GORDON, Charles George, General (1833-1885)

Man of God, Man of War . . .

Though he was born and trained in Woolwich, Kent, not surprisingly, can lay little claim to Gordon's, almost incredible military exploits in distant parts of the world. But it was in shabby Thameside Gravesend that he fought even tougher battles for the poor and needy.

As a Royal Engineers cadet at the nearby Royal Military Academy (1847) the man whose life was to be 'in the hands of God' was twice court-martialled: once for butting a corporal; once for bullying. He was however already too efficient a soldier to be dismissed the Service.

Posted to the Crimea, he distinguished himself at Sebastopol. In China he took part in the capture of Peking and witnessed the destruction of the Summer Palace. Becoming a legend, a demi-god, by sheer force of personality he welded a ruffian horde into the disciplined Ever Victorious Army. He led them, with only a cane in his hand, into 33 actions often against fortified towns and finally to victory over the Tien Wang rebels.

For such outstanding service the Chinese Government presented him with their most cherished awards: the yellow jacket . . . the peacock feather . . . and an enormous specially struck gold medal. Typically, the English made do with the Companion of the Bath, an award largely for Civil Servants who had worked blamelessly at their Whitehall desks from 10 to 4 five days a week.

For a man with adventure in his blood there could have been no greater contrast than his next posting. From heroic action in the Far East to rebuilding (expensively and uselessly) crumbling Tudor riverside fortifications at Gravesend. For all that they were 'the quietest and most peaceful days I ever knew'. During those six years his garden was always open to the sick and old; his house, to barefoot street arabs. For the former he bought food; for the latter, boots by the hundred . . . and as a result was frequently penniless until his next payday.

These ragamuffins he called his Wangs (his Kings). He taught them, advised them; found them jobs; and, above all, read to them from the only book he himself ever read, The Bible. 'I like my religious views - they are a great comfort to me' he explained.

Six years later Gordon's life changed again, equally dramatically. Another river: the Danube, to improve its navigation. Then the Nile along whose banks he built a chain of fortified posts and on whose waters, above the cataracts, he set up a steamer service. In Equatoria, unexplored, savage and pestilential, he fought to wipe out the slave trade. And to crush incipient rebellion, he made an 85 mile dash, by camel, in searing heat, with only a handful of troops.

And then, again the Sudan - and Khartoum. Here he was to die after a five month siege. To die, perhaps not unwillingly. 'I am not the rescued lamb and will not be'. The fault had been in Gladstone's dilatoriness in sending only a belated relief force. Ironically it arrived just two days after his death.

History debates whether, contemptuously unarmed, he was hacked down by the swords of Dervishes screaming 'Cursed one, your time is come!' or whether, pistol and sword in hand, still fighting, he was eventually brought down by sheer weight of numbers. But it is known that his head was put on contemptuous display by the Mahdi (whom that other great Kentish man, Winston Churchill, helped destroy at Omdurman).

In Gravesend, Chinese Gordon is remembered and portrayed in the riverside gardens on the site of the earthworks he had built. At Gillingham, in Brompton Barracks, today's Army looks up to him as he rides high on a finely sculpted and richly caparisoned camel.

GREAT DUNSTAN (1080-)

The Voice of Canterbury Cathedral . . .

BORN in honour of St Dunstan (a bell-founder himself) but very much a character in his own right. The first Great Dunstan may have been cast as far back as 1080; his alter ego in 1762. The latter's was a rather public birth for it took place, not in some discreet and distant foundry, but in the bustling Precincts themselves. A sturdy fellow for he weighed just over 3 tons!

Great Dunstan spent long years, from 1855 to 1981, not so much *in* the South-West Arundel Tower as *on* it. On the very leads - with no more protection from howling winds and lashing rain than a scanty lean-to roof. But from there his brazen voice boomed out hourly to the City sprawled below him.

In 1981, the peal of bells snugly inside the tower was scrapped to help make a majestic new ring of 14 bells hung on a steel frame given by - the Woolwich! Before they first spoke, according to old custom, they had been both blessed and baptized by Archbishop Robert Runcie: Simon, Crundale, Alphege, Thomas, Mary, Elizabeth, Anselm, Ernulf, Blaise, John, Lanfranc, Gabriel, Augustine, and 34 cwt tenor, Trinity. (To ring all the changes on them would, I'm told, take 38 years!).

At the same time Great Dunstan was transferred to the less crowded comfort of the North-West Oxford Tower together with five clock bells (and the clock mechanism) on a frame given by - the Anglia. Not that the clock face is on this tower. It is on the neighbouring south-west tower sometimes known, though erroneously) as the Clock Tower. Today Great Dunstan's voice is heard for 10 minutes each day as he urges on the laggard faithful to 8 o'clock Eucharist.

Which sadly says nothing of the oldest of them all (1635), the venerable 8 cwt Bell Harry on his own magnificently pinnacled tower.

In 1988, the 1000th anniversary of Saint Dunstan's death, Great Dunstan unhappily developed a crack (rheumatism?) in his shoulder. With infinite care, befitting his age, he was lowered to the Nave floor to be sent away to a Whitechapel foundry for the finest modern technological treatment - and to be in time to add his mighty voice to the paeans of praise raised to the memory of that good Saint.

For all that Great Dunstan fared much better than some of his forbears. *They* were hung in a campanile on a slight mound near the South-West transept. In May 1382, a playful earthquake shook down its six bells! But not for another 300 years was the tottering bell tower demolished!

HARRYS, Richard

Fruiterer to the King . . .

IT MUST always be remembered - and blessed at that - that in 1533 (catering perhaps for Henry VIII's taste for ripeness in fruit as well as in women) Richard Harrys did 'plant by his great costs and rare industrie the sweet Cherry, the temperate Pippen, and the golden Reinette'.

HARVEY, William (1587-1657)

Physician Extraordinary . . .

THE man who gained a European reputation by revolutionising 17th century ideas on physiology as radically as contempories Copernicus and Galileo did astronomy, was born in Folkestone.

He first saw light of day in Church Street, at Post House, 'fair built of stone'. Born on 1st April - but most certainly no fool. His much propertied father's ancestors included a Mayor of London.

William was first educated at King's School, Canterbury. Then at Caius College, Cambridge, a college even then with a bias towards medicine which now fascinated him. Years later he obtained for it an invaluable charter: the annual gift of the bodies of two criminals which, after dissection, were buried by Master and Fellows with ritual ceremony.

Next, a far cry, he went to Padua University in Northern Italy. Here he sparred physically, as well as mentally, with the best student brains in Europe; was taught by the anatomist Hieronymus Fabricius, and was influenced by Galileo, philosopher and astronomer. In 1602 he emerged as a fully fledged Doctor of Medicine.

On his return to England he shrewdly married a Court Physician's daughter and equally shrewdly himself became a Physician Extraordinary to James I. Later he loyally followed Charles I to Oxford and in 1642, before the Battle of Edgehill, was entrusted with the care of the future Charles II. Together they sheltered under a thick hedge with Harvey calmly reading aloud to him until Roundhead cannonades, coming too close for comfort, 'forced him to move his station'.

At the end of the Civil War, during his exile from London because of his Royalist sympathies, his rooms were vandalised by ignorant soldiery. The painstaking notes he had made over years were destroyed in as many minutes. 'It was the most crucifying loss I ever knew.' In appearance, Aubrey recounts, he was 'of the lowest stature; olive complexion; little eyes, round, very black, full of spirit; hair black as a raven's wing'. Spirit indeed! He was aggressive, certainly did not suffer fools gladly, and on occasion drew a knife from his belt to emphasise his point of argument.

At Barts and the College of Physicians he dissected not only human cadavers but also those of every wild creature he could lay hands on. Lovingly he enjoined his anatomy students to 'study closely the lower belly; nasty but recompensed by admirable variety'; as well as 'the divine banquet of the brain'. He turned grocers into respected apothecaries with their own Society but treated surgeons as little more than old time barber-surgeons, fit only for blood letting. Gradually, by shrewd observation, he formulated his famous hypothesis: 'That blood flowed into the heart via the arteries and out of it, to be re-oxygenated, and then returned through the veins'. Later, as assistant he briefly had a talented young model maker: one, 15 year old Christopher Wren.

This revolutionary concept 'On the Motion of the Heart and Blood' ('Exertatis Anatomica de Motu Cardis and Sanguinis') was published, graphically illustrated, in 1628, when he was 50. But it was greeted with much scepticism for it was not based on 'ancient authority' and it went against the theories of Galen, noted 2nd Century physiologist, and physician to gladiators!

'A crackpot idea' sneered his jealous peers. 'Find another less dangerous doctor' they urged his fearful patients. But Harvey lived to see his ideas accepted. And, in addition, in 1651, to write, in bad Latin and in 72 chapters 'Generatione Animalium' on the generative process of animals. Excellent anatomist though he was, it was held that his workaday prescriptions 'were not worth threepence: for from them could not be told what he did aim at'.

In private life, Harvey was, to say the least, eccentric. 'Man', he maintained, 'is but a great mischievous baboon'. He had caves dug in which he could meditate for he swore he could comtemplate best in the dark; When he could not sleep he paced his chamber until he was seized by a shivering fit. In winter, for his gout, he resorted to his roof to freeze his legs in buckets of icy water and then roast them by a hot stove indoors.

A little more conventionally he kept a pretty young wench to wait on him - and at nights made use of her for warmth. After all, wasn't he only following the aged King David's example. She obviously gave satisfaction for he remembered her in his Will.

A Beauteous virgin still enjoyed by none
Nor seen unveiled by anyone.
When Harvey's violent passion she did see
Began to tremble and to flee.
Took Sancturary like Daphne in a tree:
There Daphne's lover stop't and thought it much
The very leaves of her to touch.
But Harvey, our Apollo, stop't not so,
Into the Bark, and root he after her did goe'
Abraham Cowley, 'Ode to Dr Harvey'

With his brother, Eliab, who was one of the first to import coffee beans, at a very fair profit, he drank much of the ever more popular beverage that 'comforted the Brain and Heart and helped Digestion'.

His gift of a handsome museum and library (for which he sold land near Hythe at Burmarsh) was tragically destroyed within years by the Great Fire. But today William Harvey himself stands high on Folkestone Leas, deer's heart in one hand; his own beneath the other.

Hasted related that he died tragically - by his own hand. Dreading blindness he always kept a bottle of poison in his room - and when with blinds and shutters flung open by his housekeeper he could see no light, he straightway drained it.

HEATH, Edward R. G. (1916-)

Prime Minister, musician, sailor . . .

UNASSUMING Broadstairs, Dickens' favourite watering place, was also the birthplace of a baby destined to lead the British people. Not only born there but educated at the village school before he moved on to Chatham House Grammar School, Margate. He was musician before he was M.P. On early family visits to his grandparents he precociously enjoyed the sing-songs round the piano to uproarious games of whist or rummy which bored him.

And when only 9 years old he was introduced by his parents to the love of his life - an ill-afforded Thornton Bobby piano, costing the then not inconsiderable sum of £42. 'Stick at your practising' urged his father. 'It will be the joy of your life.' He did just that - and it still is. It served him well for 40 years until as Premier he had a Steinway installed at No 10 in the White Drawing Room overlooking Horse Guards Parade.

It led him also to the choir at St Peter's, Broadstairs - and to 1½d each practice and 2½d for each Sunday service. So that it should not be frittered away each week (or was it to encourage regular attendance?) it was paid only at the end of three months.

Of all the hymns he sang 'Blessed be the God and Father of Our Lord Jesus Christ' was, as a treble soloist, his favourite. He also loved Vaughan William's magnificent setting for 'For all the Saints' but, not yet fully aware of the niceties of punctuation, was long puzzled by:

'Through countless gates of pearl stream
In the countless host.'

He was a leading member too of the informal Our Carol Party which sang in the open no matter how hard the wind was blowing or the snow whirling across the North Foreland.

An organ scholarship to Oxford's Balliol led to his first moves in diplomacy: a tactful and flattering letter to the Mayor himself asking for his essential support for the formation of an official Town Carol Concert. It became a very well established event to which he unfailingly returned years after he had risen from President of the Oxford Union to Prime Minister of the United Kingdom. One to which, at his invitation came Sir Malcolm Sargent to help increase the funds for summer holidays and Christmas presents for deprived children.

Membership of the Broadstairs Sailing Club was a foretaste of his second love, sailing. Small beer perhaps compared with his later acquired ocean-going skills: winner of the Sydney-Hobart Race; Commodore of the victorious British team which won the world famous Admiral's Cup. His 'Sailing', hailed as a triumphantly lavish book, was destined to become a record breaking best seller of its kind.

Today, after 45 years in the Commons the small boy who invariably chose Mr Creasy's pigs' chitterlings, liver and trotters as his birthday treat, is a silver-haired, generously jowled *eminence grise* "the cranky old sod", of a torn and tattered Conservative Party which he has served for 60 years; the man who led us into the European Common Market.

HENGIST - AND HORSA
(Hengist died 488 AD; Horsa, 455 AD)

Stallion - and Gelding . . .

VERY definitely not a knock-about comedy team . . . but semi-legendary Jutish brothers and warriors. Their story starts, so the 'Saxon Chronicle' tells us, with Vortigern, king of the Britons. Frighteningly naive, the latter did not see the mountain of troubles he was laying up in store for himself when he invited such mercenaries to help him drive back the marauding Dark Age invaders, the Picts and Scots.

In 449 they landed in three fierce, dragon-prowed longships at Pegwell Bay near Ebbsfleet. And for their future pains were given the Isle of Thanet. (1500 years later their first arrival was celebrated when 20th century Jutes rowed the 'Hugin' across the North Sea to Pegwell Bay - and left it there for us as a splendid and unusual memorial). Not so naive as Vortigern, Hengist quickly noticed 'the choice nature of the land and the worthlessness of the Britons'. Straightway he sent home not only for fighting reinforcements but also for women and children to settle the land. More diplomatically, he gave his daughter, Rowena, in marriage to Vortigern.

The Jutes made short work of the King's enemies. And then a few years later in 455 AD they turned on Vortigern at Aylesford. (20th century

Odin worshippers are currently contesting, doubtless with legal aid, the passage of the billion pound, Channel Tunnel rail-link through a nearby holy spot).

Horsa was killed in the battle; some historians tentatively suggest it was at the hands of his brother who wanted no rival. But Hengist and his son, Aesc, unperturbed, again turned on their masters at Creganford (Crayford) 'destroying four companies by fire and the sword's edge'. Defeated, Vortigern's people retreated north to London 'in great fear, and yielded up Kent'.

Over the next ten years land-hungry Hengist, King of Kent, turned his unwelcome attention on the Welsh. In battle, amongst many others, one of his own thanes, Wipped, and 12 of the Welsh Ealdormen were killed. 'Countless spoils of war were seized and the Welsh fled as one flees fire.'

Today, Hengist's name lives on in the 3,200 line saga of that still mightier warrior, Beowulf, who, with 14 chosen companions, first killed the monster Grendel, then, under water beheaded his vengeful water-hag mother!

HOWLEY, Dr William, Archbishop of Canterbury (1766-1848)

Enthroned by Proxy ... !

HOWLEY, as Archbishop of Canterbury, had been at the bedside of William IV, the Sailor King, when he died. And as such he was deputed, together with the Lord Chamberlain, to drive post-haste to tell Princess Victoria that she was Princess no longer, but Queen (1837). As they arrived early in the morning they had to browbeat sleepy and frightened servants even to obtain admission to Kensington Palace. And it was only after fierce altercation that the formidable Duchess of Kent could be persuaded to break 'the sweet sleep' of the young woman, now a Queen. And he was, of course, to crown her.

So much for the good but there was much on the 'flip' side too. Much the citizens of Canterbury did not like. He had indeed robbed his people of the rich ceremonial (and financial pickings) of his enthronement. Instead of coming to the City in person he had, believe it or not, sent down a proxy by the mundane old Canterbury fly!

Almost worse, he had spoken in the Lords, though spoken very badly, against National Education, against Catholic Relief, and even against the Reform Bill. By opposition to the latter, Canterburians felt that he may have cost many of them the vote. And that he had also reduced the marriage rights of a Freeman's daughter and thereby her hopes of a generous dowry.

As compensatory Fate had it, he was shortly after to attend the conventional banquet with the Mayor and Corporation at the Guildhall. Honest citizens wanted none of it. An advance party, unable to restrain their emotions, hurried out to greet him at Harbledown to let him know their feelings. A wiser man would have turned back. But Archbishop Howley was not a wise man. Outside the Guildhall the gentry lined up to greet him. So, unfortunately, did the lower and middle classes.

They came armed with fresh fruit and stale fish - and a dead cat. Inaccurately aimed, it struck his Chaplain who complained bitterly of such rude hospitality. Of sympathy for him, Howley, though normally a generous man, had none. 'Be grateful it wasn't a live one!'.

Constables were swept aside and the mob chanted with all the zest of modern Kop fans,' 'Drag him out! Drag him out!'

A magistrate vainly called to the infuriated crowd, 'Desist from such cowardly and disgraceful conduct'; slammed shut the timorously half-opened carriage door, and urged 'Drive to the Deanery.' Excited outriders and whips forced a way through the mob but headed down St Margaret's Street instead of Mercery Lane. It was left to a Canterbury-born footman to save the day by heading the horses - and the Archbishop - to safety in the Deanery.

Humble pie figured largely on the following day's menu. 'The Archbishop', wrote the Mayor, 'stands high in the estimation of all respectable citizens who bitterly regret the previous evening's disgraceful and undignified occasion.' Despite such an apology, William Howley, Archbishop of Canterbury never again visited the City or his Cathedral.

What good can be said of the poor man? That, with Mrs Howley's not inconsiderable help, he spent £60,000 modernising the more welcome Lambeth Palace? That no woman was allowed to set foot in it except on social occasions? And that with Evensong Chapel over, preceded by men carrying flambeaux, he dutifully retired to Mrs Howley's lodgings?

He was indeed a pacific man; one of remarkable gentleness, with only a single blemish on his character. As a schoolboy at Winchester he had, when cunningly checkmated by one Sidney Smith, been so incensed that he had struck him over the head with the chess-board.

'The gentlest and wisest Archbishop of the century' said social reformer, Robert Chadwick. 'The biggest fool alive' retorted Lord Melbourne with even more certainty. The choice is yours, O reader.

JAGGER, Mick (1943 -)

Rock group king . . .

EVERYONE KNOWS 'a rolling stone gathers no moss'. This one, however, seems likely to. Now 51, in search of peace and quiet, he has been interestedly eyeing Chilham Castle. At a cool £3,000,000 (reduced price) it's a definite bargain that would go well with houses in London, New York, Paris and Mustique.

With it are thrown in a ghostly White Lady; and the much more recent shades of Lovejoy and Poirot, both of whom filmed here. Hopefully, some at least of his covey of 'chicks' won't come home to roost. But if the Chilham herons don't do so by St Valentine's Day, legend prophesies disaster will strike the castle towers.

As Jagger is Dartford born it will, after his world orbits (nearly as frequent as a satellite's) surely be a matter of the Prodigal's Return to Kent.

JEZREEL, James Jershom (Died 1885)

The Sixth Trumpeter of God . . .

HE WAS simply and poorly born as James White; enlisted in 1875, in the 16th Regiment of Foot; and was posted to Chatham. There he also enlisted, more wholeheartedly, in the Christian Israalite sect.

Though promotion evaded him in the army his fervour in religion saw him become leader - of his own splinter group, the New and Latter House of Israel. The Army however took no account of such things and callously posted him far from Kent to India. There he suffered more from the barbed raillery of his bawdy and blasphemous comrades than he did from Pathan attack. Dismissed as 'of indifferent character' he returned to England and Chatham.

Here he showed character enough to have startled even the War Office. A bold frontal attack won him the hand of his neighbour's 21 year old daughter, Clarissa Rogers . . . and also a corrugated iron shed. In this he led services which would have delighted today's trendies. Clarissa played the harp; children, 'out of the mouths of babes and sucklings', preached sermons; and 'virgins' washed 'saints' feet.

Open air meetings attracted 2,000 or more curious citizens. A steadily growing number were converted and became Jezreelites. All their wealth and goods had to be handed over to the sect. In return they were promised that 144,000 would be saved when the world shortly ended. And that instant immortality would be theirs. Meantime the leader had changed workaday James White into impressive Old Testament character, Jezreel.

Tours of America, by horse and waggon, drew a disappointingly small return but some trans-atlantic cousins did come to Chatham and others at least contributed to the sect's ever growing financial funds - shrewdly invested locally by Jezreel.

In a vision he was commanded to build a chapel near Fort Darland. The War Office - again - put a curt stop to that. Undefeated, Jezreel settled for a site high on Chatham Hill beside the main London road. It was to be no mean building.

He planned the Tower for the Second Coming as a 144 ft cube with four striking corner towers. It even incorporated such modern novelties as gas and electricity. But its greatest wonder was its central hall, able to hold 5,000 fervent worshippers beneath a dome 90 ft above them. In its midst was planned a hydraulically operated platform that would not only rise up 30 feet but also revolve so that all might clearly see the preacher. Sadly however Jezreel was not to see the fulfilment of his dream.

It was Clarissa who on his death fought off challengers for the leadership and who at last got the building under way. But the now self-styled Queen Esther also developed an irrestisible desire for clothes and for a smart carriage and pair. The latter she drove with such scant regard for her own safety - or for that of others - that she must undeniably have believed in immortality.

She too was not to see the completion of the Tower for she died, not in a horrendous clash with another carriage, but from peritonitis. Hitherto generously given funds were by now running low and not being replenished. In 1901 the Jezreelites were evicted from their half-finished tower. Sadly 'Pearls of truth had been offered to many but few had received them'.

It was not until some 60 years later that despite spirited opposition to the demolition of their unique landmark by local residents its destruction began. It took 14 months and an accidental death (the fulfilment of Jezreel's curse on anyone seeking his tower's destruction?) to raze it to the ground. And for the building destined to be a stairway to heaven to become the foundation of the new Medway Bridge near Rochester.

JOY, Richard (Died 1742)

A Kent Samson . . .

LIVING in the early 18th century he carried the banner for other Broadstairs greats to follow: Heath and Harmsworth, Crampton and Sickert . . .

He lifted huge stones as if they were pebbles; tore in two a rope which would bear 35 cwt; and unmoved, pulled against 'an Extraordinary Strong Horse'. Had he had a modern impresario he might long have continued to be the star turn in all Thanet. But his acts were as few as his exaggerated claims were many. Local interest waned.

To London - and a Royal Command performance before William III! But his new-found public was as fickle as his old. So it was back to Broadstairs to hump barrels of contraband French brandy - until he was drowned in the course of duty! And, for all that, was buried in St Peter's graveyard.

KITCHENER, Horatio Herbert, 1st Earl Kitchener of Khartoum (1850 - 1916)

Man with a Mission . . .

THE MAN who was to save England after the B.E.F., 'that contemptible little army' had been overrun in the early days of World War I, was born not in England but in Ireland's County Kerry.

After education in Switzerland, however, he came to Kent. In 1871, as a young man, he studied at the Royal Military Academy at Woolwich and at the Royal Engineers HQ at Brompton, near Chatham. Many years later, still a confirmed bachelor, he made his home at Broome Park, near Canterbury.

His early Army years were spent with a French Ambulance Unit and, more mundanely, as Intelligence Officer in Palestine, Anatolia and Cyprus. However, in 1885, it was as Sirdah, Commander-in-Chief, of the British Army and of the Nile Expeditionary Force driving through the Sudan to rescue the desperately beleaguered General Gordon that he made his real mark. Through the gross dilatoriness of Gladstone in dispatching the relieving force rather than through any failing of his own, despite all his fierce drive, he reached Khartoum just two days too late. Gordon had been murdered!

Revenge had to exacted. After building a railway (he was not an R.E. for nothing) and organising a flotilla of gunboats, Kitchener exacted it in full with an angry ruthlessness. At Omdurman he was heavily outnumbered by frenzied Dervishes. But ancient swords, outdated muskets, and fanatical courage were no match for light artillery, small arms, the newly invented lethal machine-gun, and iron discipline. Seemingly destroyed, the Mahdi's troops suddenly rallied dangerously. Only a death or glory charge by the 21st Lancers swung them back into a panic-stricken rout. It was on Kitchener's order that this fleeing rabble were mercilessly cut down. So great was the massacre that some 25,000 Dervishes were killed or wounded: a fate suffered by only 500 of his English troops. For such a victory his reward was public acclamation, a peerage, and a generous Government reward which later enabled him to settle in Kent in some style.

The same Draconian tactics brought him success in the Boer War. After public clamour he took over command from 'Bobs', the 1st Earl Roberts; a V.C. and of Indian Mutiny and Relief of Lucknow fame. Kitchener worked with methodical ruthlessness. He never attacked unless he had superiority in numbers; set up chains of block-houses; burnt settlements; and took the war to women and children whom he drove into concentration camps to end their covert help. Concentration camps, not filled with the cold evil of Hitler's hells, but bleak and disease ridden enough to cause many deaths. Victory followed. Lord Kitchener became Lord Viscount Kitchener.

His name was made. His next step up the ladder was as Commander- in- Chief of the Armies in India. Here his main enemy was not rebellious tribes but a single man - the Viceroy himself. In their private war, Kitchener was the broadsword: Viscount Curzon, the rapier. To such a man as Kitchener, it was intolerable that he did not have the final responsibility for military decisions. Curzon fought bitterly to retain control but the broadsword was too powerful and he was forced to resign (1902 - 09).

The Viceroyalty surely now lay open to the man on the spot. The man who with his recognised 'Thoroughness' had reorganised the Army from top to bottom, starting and finishing, it is said, with the Quartermaster's Stores! Bitterly disappointed however, Kitchener was passed over - to become instead virtual ruler of Egypt - and an Earl.

Came World War I. And now the Asquith Government *did* turn to him as Secretary for War. He 'played Hell' at the War Office, blasting those who fatuously talked of an early victory. 'Three years' he warned them, 'Three years, no less, to build the huge army that alone can crush the Germans'. It was largely his charisma and drive that brought the necessary tens of thousands of patriotic young men flocking to the colours - and to the carnage of the Somme. So too did 'that famous poster': Kitchener's stabbing finger, his hypnotic eyes; and the message 'Your Country Needs YOU'.

To keep them on the straight and narrow path of rectitude, he urged them, in their paybooks: 'Do your duty. Fear God. Honour the King'. And, in only slightly smaller print, 'Resist the temptation of both wine and women.' Shrewd strategy indeed for where else would Tommy Atkins read as regularly and eagerly? But surely in the face of death, an optimistic one.

In all, Kitchener raised and trained 67 infantry divisions, including the 'Pals' Divisions which, to boost morale allowed men from the same town or village to serve together. Too often, however, it resulted in a village thrown into mourning after losing half its young men in one ill-conceived offensive.

As the War ground on, both Government and War Office colleagues lost their blind faith in him. Admittedly it was impossible to improve on his 'Thorough' administration but his wider strategies were called into question. The Premier, Lloyd George, once an ardent admirer, now likened him to a revolving lighthouse, 'spreading momentary glimpses of light before relapsing into complete darkness'.

By now he had bought Broome Park, mid-way between Canterbury and Folkestone. Here, for snatched days, he could forget the almost intolerable strains and stresses of ordering a nation's men to war. And it was from here, in 1916, that he set off for Scapa Flow in the far North. There he boarded the cruiser HMS 'Hampshire' waiting for him with steam up to take him to Russia so that his drive might keep a wavering, broken nation in the War. Off The Orkneys, only two hours after slipping out into the open sea, the 'Hampshire' struck a mine . . . Erect and unemotional as ever, Kitchener was last seen standing on the upper deck wordlessly awaiting his end.

Austere in social life, severe of countenance, harsh in the face of opposition, he had always driven his officers and men hard - but never harder than he drove himself. He was a man with an overwhelming sense of duty and mission. The nation mourned the loss of an idol but cynical Press magnate, Lord Harmsworth cruelly gloated, 'At last Providence is on our side'.

Broome Park, built by Inigo Jones, is one of the finest examples of a Jacobean redbrick mansion in the whole of Southern England. In its grounds, the Minister for War turned Gardener and so perforce did even his most eminent guests; and General turned Scoutmaster with youngsters camping in its rolling parkland. Today (now a Country Club) its magnificent Great Hall is lined with paintings of him in the medal starred uniform of the Khedive; mounted, sword aloft waving his troops forward at Omdurman; grim faced, dictating terms to grizzled Boers. And above the overmantel of one of its vast fireplaces, is the single word by which he lived - 'Thorough'.

LANFRANC (1005-1089)

Builder of a Cathedral . . .

JUST after the turn of the first millenium a baby boy was born in the city of Pavia lying in the distant shadow of the Italian Alps. He was of no great import - except, of course, to his mother. Certainly no one would have guessed that he was to become, via the abbeys of Bec and of Caen, Primate of All England. And that he would build in Canterbury the finest Cathedral in Europe; and bring unity to a divided Church.

Nearly 70, he seemed a strange choice for so demanding a task. Not that, as far as he was concerned, there had been very much choice about it. William the Conqueror, for all his illiteracy, knew a truly great man when he met one: 'Respected him as a father; venerated him as a priest; and loved him as a brother'. He had already summarily deposed Anglo-Saxon Archbishop Stigand and imprisoned him at Winchester - where he died. So William desperately needed the Abbot of Caen as Archbishop of Canterbury.

Lanfranc pleaded, vainly, 'I am too old. I am ignorant of the customs and language of these most barbaric people'. William was unmoved. 'The Church needs you. You are the man most fitted for the office. You must accept'.

So, in 1070, Lanfranc had come to Canterbury. Come to a Saxon Cathedral that fire had hungrily devoured just three years before; and to a lax and demoralised brotherhood of monks. So the Abbot from Caen's imposing monastery was consecrated Archbishop of a stricken Cathedral, in a makeshift shelter. He wrote to the Pope: 'All around me I see such sorrow, such harshness, such evil that I weary of life'. That said, 'the most energetic and honourable man' with fervent determination started to build anew. First, neglecting his own urgent need for accommodation, 'he completed in all haste the houses of the monks. (But for all that he was not to live in their midst as his predecessors had for centuries - but to have his own palace). More importantly, he gave them a wise constitution; and instituted the Benedictine Rules of worship and labour; of poverty, chastity and obedience.

Equally important, by the Accord of Winchester, he gave the whole Church stability under one Head. There the Primacy of Canterbury was formally if bitterly recognised. The historic document, which can still be seen in Canterbury Cathedral's library, was signed under the Great Seal and witnessed by the King - with an X - the Papal Legate, six bishops - and the vaunting Archbishop of York. Only after long and bitter debate did the latter write 'Concedo' and sign beneath it. No longer could each bishop be a law unto himself. There was a new unity in the Church.

So too, because little was left, Lanfranc swept away the ruins of the old Cathedral and built anew from its very foundations. Its width and length were much the same as those of today's nave. It was of eight bays:

four serving as nave for the people's Church; four as Choir where the monks could carry out their own rituals of prayer and praise. One was separated from the other by the Great Rood upon which stood Christ crucified, amid angels, and with the Virgin Mary and St John on either side.

Externally there rose two Western towers (of which the Norman one stood firm for over 800 years until, in 1832, it had to be demolished to have sturdy Norman lines changed to soaring Gothic). And each shone brilliantly with gilded pinnacles. Above all rose the Central Tower, the Angel Steeple, on which stood a six-winged seraph: 'with twain he covered his face; and with twain his feet; and with twain he did fly'. It was to become the joyous inspiration of pilgrims as they wearily breasted Harbledown Hill on the last stage of their journey - and saw the Cathedral towering protectively over the City below them.

'For seen with gilded seraph crowned
This shrine is Britain's holiest ground.'
John of Salisbury

Yet within 30 years, Lanfranc's Choir, and Crypt below it, were as nothing: both had been demolished. Not by Viking invaders but by the monastery's own devoted Prior Ernulf, a monk there for 26 years. With a steadily increasing number of brethren, the small Choir had been outgrown. So, in a bare 12 years, Ernulf built a much greater one, 190' long and with an impressive crypt beneath it. Whilst the latter is rightly known as Ernulf's Crypt, the former is his successor Conrad's 'Glorious Choir'. 'Glorious' for its golden cross; its gilded chandelier; its treasure chests filled with the relics of saints; its wealth of colour in its bright murals, rich arras, and bejewelled ornaments. Its dedication, in 1130, was held to be the most splendid since Solomon's Temple! Even so this did not spare it from a still greater conflagration in 1174, shortly after Henry II had done penance at Becket's tomb.

Lanfranc was 84 when he died. He had left Canterbury with a gleaming new Cathedral of white Caen stone, shipped up the narrow Stour to nearby Fordwich; probably the first ever organised Hospital, at St John's in Northgate, and a reputation for openhanded generosity, giving as much as £500 a year to beggars. Today he sleeps, contentedly one hopes, in the North East transept in St Martin's Chapel.

MYNN, Alfred (1807-1861)

The Very Best Bowler in England . . .

"**K**IND AND MANLY" Alfred Mynn was a giant in every sense of the word. 6 ft 1 in in his stockinged feet, and tipping the beam with 17 stone of bone and muscle, he was every ounce and inch a typical Kentish yeoman farmer. Generally he took the field in 'a close fitting jersey bound with red, blue belt round his waist and a straw hat with a red ribbon on his head'. A splendid figure of a man!

Short though his run up to the wicket was, he dug a grave with a pile-driver left foot. It was the batsman's grave, not his, for he bowled 'thundering destructives'. Gloveless wicket-keepers of his day preferred to let one of the *two* longstops earn his keep rather than 'knock his own hands to pieces'. As a batsman he could hit a ball as lustily as he bowled it.

If Mynn's heart was as big as a balloon, his hands were certainly like small shoulders of mutton. He looked 'fit enough to carry the church, and the whole congregation too, round the town'.

Above all, he enjoyed the cut and thrust of single-wicket matches. He refused to play against his friend and team mate, Fuller Pilch, for fear of creating ill-feeling. But he had no qualms in twice beating Dearman, the 'Yorkshire Terrier', by handsome margins. Even so the Tyke was cheered off the field as lustily as the Kent Lion; not for his bottle but, same thing, 'for his bottom' in unflinchingly taking much punishment.

In those days bumpers reared head high as regularly as they do today. But then they were caused by 'pitch' rather than by 'pitcher'. On one unforgettable occasion, when he scored 125* for South v North, he was so badly battered by Redgate that after the match he had to be hoisted onto the roof of the Kent coach like some giant ungainly parcel. After an agonising journey he was off-loaded early at Barts Hospital in London. 'You may amputate my foot if you must but I would sooner die than lose the whole limb' he told anxiously debating surgeons. After second and third thoughts they put the very idea out of their heads. And eventually saved Alfred Mynn for Kent cricket.

He was an iron man indeed. What other bowler would have said, 'For myself I should like a *hundred* balls in an over'? What other player, in jest, could pick up a lively colleague, Felix, with one hand - and hold him dangling in mid-air?

All too often in debt, Mynn was farmer and hop-merchant in Goudhurst and Town Malling. He trained, in order of importance, on beef and beer. But it was with a tankard of the latter in one hand and a Bible in the other that he would make his way to bed.

He was buried, with richly deserved military honours, beside his daughter in the garden graveyard of Thurnham (near Maidstone) with the Downs above it to keep an eye on this greatest of all Kent cricketers.

NAPOLEON, Louis (1808-1873)

Emperor who fled to Kent . . .

IT IS hard to imagine unsung Chislehurst boasting not merely a member of the Imperial House of Bonaparte but an Emperor of the French to boot. Almost as hard to realise that one of this Frenchman's favourite recreations was to watch Kentish cricket!

As a youngster he attended a college in Augsburg. His holidays however were divided between his father (appointed King of Holland by Napoleon Bonaparte himself) in his decaying Florentine palace; and his mother in her castle on the shores of Lake Constance. His youthful, idealistic support for a Liberal revolution and his own bravery in an abortive attack on Civita Castellone in Romagna led to his mother having to smuggle him hurriedly out of danger dressed as one of her footmen . . . And so to Dover and Kent, the first of several such visits.

After a horrendously rough crossing, unsympathetic Dover greeted them with torrential rain. Canterbury was in the throes of a noisy and bitter Reform Bill election. So his mother, Queen Hortense, sought relief for her jangled nerves in the healing waters and bracing air of Tunbridge Wells.

Louis found his in the arms of a Miss Godfrey, 'as beautiful as she was accomplished'. Their enforced parting when he returned to London left him wracked with 'long sighs fit to turn the sails of a windmill'. But . . . like many other such encounters it came to nothing for he was notoriously inconstant.

In 1836, he made a disastrous attempt, at Strasbourg, to overthrow the Orleanist government. It failed miserably but he received no worse punishment than a brief exile in America. Undeterred by one failure, in 1840 he tried again. This was to prove an even damper squib than his first effort, even though it had a Kentish tang.

His followers were temporarily lodged in Sevenoaks; the 'Edinburgh Castle' loaded flags and proclamations, guns and pistols, horses and carriages, and, of course, wines and food, at Deptford. More recruits were taken aboard at Greenwich. And Louis himself, rather belatedly, because in London he had been forced to evade French Embassy surveillance, at Gravesend. Finally, at Ramsgate, the military leader, General Montholon, had to be woken up before they could head for Boulogne. The 'revolution' was over almost before it started.

This time it was no slap on the wrist for Louis. Rather, he was sentenced to imprisonment 'in perpetuity' in the grim fortress of Ham, set amid the desolate marshes of the Somme. Defiantly he turned prison into University, writing treatises on such diverse subjects as the growing of sugar beet, the extinction of pauperism and, a whisker ahead of De Lesseps and the Panama, a canal across Nicaragua! After five years he snapped his fingers at perpetuity and walked out unquestioned -

disguised as a builder's labourer and with a plank on his shoulder! He arrived in London - with his dog Ham - on Derby Day.

Back again in England he enjoyed London life to the full. This included rapturously attending 15 of Jenny Lind's (the Swedish Nightingale) first 21 performances; reviewing the Royal Horse Guards at Woolwich, and, above all, bumping, almost literally, into Miss Howard.

He spotted her outside the Haymarket Theatre Royal, hesitantly stepping out into a London pea-souper; gallantly volunteered to escort her home; and for his trouble was rewarded with a somewhat niggardly pour-boire. Who was the more surprised the next day is a debatable point. She, on learning that she had tipped a member of the Blood Royal with a mere half-crown (12½p) . . .

. . . Or he, on learning that she was a shoemaker's daughter whose not inconsiderable wealth had been acquired, so whispered scandalous rumour, as a Tottenham Court Road streetwalker; as the mistress of Jack Johnstone, 'the most noted blackleg of his day; of Jack Fitzroy, 'gambler and cheat'; of Jem Mason, who much more respectably had won the first Grand National in 1839 on Lottery; and of a Major Mountjoy Martyn of the 2nd Life Guards . . . Currently unattached, she was vetting a short list of eager protectors who included a Duke and a Lord, both, of course, wealthy. Louis, besotted by her exquisite features, graceful carriage and magnificent shoulders, won the day.

This, even though, in 1851, he was courting an equally lovely creature. One born in Granada, the daughter of a Countess, and 'of surpassing beauty': the russet-haired Eugenie de Montigo, painted by the artist Winterhalter. She became his Empress, in 1853, shortly after he had engineered a legal coup in Paris. Miss Howard was, not unnaturally, furious but swiftly mollified by the title Duchesse de Beauregard and an estate near Versailles.

'Poléon, Poléon,
Nous l'aurons, nous l'aurons'

Had chanted the mob. And he had moved triumphantly into the Elysée Palace: the first President of the Second French Republic (1848). And in 1851, on the anniversary of Austerlitz, he was proclaimed Emperor of the French!

A State visit to London followed. Dover, richly decorated, and sporting a tunnel of triumphal arches was mist-shrouded. Cannons on the Castle heights and on the anchored fleet boomed as Louis was welcomed by Prince Albert when 'Pelican' drew alongside Admiralty Pier. The Mayor in his exuberance so far forgot himself as to give the signal for the staccato clapping of Kentish Fire but was abjectly overruled by protocol, etiquette and the Prince's painfully shocked entourage. The rail journey from Dover to - not Waterloo - but the Bricklayer's Arms station was one continuous ovation through the villages of Kent.

England and France fought as allies in the Crimea. For 17 years Louis ruled both wisely (bread for the workers and Baron Haussmann's face lift for Paris) - and despotically (gagging the Press and using bloody repression against the workers). He survived an attempted assassination. His major error was in goading Germany, in 1870, into a war they relished. Unfortunately Louis' mobilization of troops was as slow and inept as Germany's was swift and efficient.

Louis, having briefly assumed command, found himself outnumbered, ougunned and out-manoeuvred at Sedan. Helpless, 80,000 French troops laid down their arms; and Louis surrendered to the King of Prussia. With German soldiers marching down the Champs Elysée (only to march back again two days later) and peace signed, Louis, almost mockingly, was freed from Wilhelmshofe . . .

Was free to travel to England . . . to Dover . . . There, once again, sympathetic crowds cheered him warmly. And, on Admiralty Pier, he had a touching reunion with his wife and son, Prince Napoleon, who had prudently fled from France before final defeat.

In the previous months, the Empress had scoured the South for their enforced retirement home. She found it in Kent. So, peaceful Chislehurst was able to boast that, as fellow villagers, they had an Emperor and an Empress! For only £200 p.a. she had rented Camden House, an imposing Georgian mansion (named after the famous antiquary). It lay in its own large grounds with wide views to Chislehurst Woods, Common, Cricket Ground, and windmill.

The Emperor took little part in village affairs. But he did delight in watching the West Kent Cricket Club for, surprisingly, he had enjoyed seeing the game played in the Bois de Boulogne in Paris! On one occasion he was so thrilled by long on's sprinting and diving catch in front of his seat that a member of his retinue was sent to beg that the performance be repeated!

For the rest, the Emperor walked in the grounds of Camden House, across the Common, even as far as St Paul's Cray - and the awed village children soon found that his pockets held seemingly unending pennies. Indoors, he wrote and studied as he had at Ham and worked on a small lathe.

In late December, 1873, he suffered severe pain from a large stone in his bladder. London surgeons were hastily summoned and, on an old iron bedstead doubling as an operating table, it was removed. Nevertheless, he grew weaker - only 'une petite crise' averred the experts - but it was one big enough to end his life. His last words: 'We weren't cowards at Sedan, were we?'.

In his final journey across the Common to the Catholic Church of St Mary he was escorted by a huge concourse. Leading the procession marched a deputation of Parisian workman carrying an improvised Tricolour. Behind the hearse paced French admirals and generals, ministers and senators, representatives of the British Royal Family, a small army of French exiles, the local gentry . . . and hundreds of mourning villagers. Chislehurst had never seen anything like it.

But Louis was not to rest in Kent. The Empress, haunted by Camden House's painful memories, moved away to Farnborough Hill. Having bought a house there, from Thomas Longman, the publisher, she instructed Gabriel Destailler to build a remarkable 16th century French flamboyant church over a Romanesque crypt.

In the latter, in red Scottish marble sarcophagi were laid the bodies of Louis and his son, Prince Napoleon (who had been educated at Woolwich and St Cyr). Though a non-combatant, he had died in the Zulu War . . . from 14 assegai thrusts when a broken stirrup-leather prevented his escape.

The Empress who had chosen Kent and Chislehurst as her first sanctuary lived on to be 94! Then was buried beside her husband and son.

NASH, Richard (Beau) (1674-1762)

Welsh Dandy . . .

HE WAS half-educated at Oxford, which he left in a hurry with a lady not far behind; commissioned in the Guards; called to the Bar . . . only to sacrifice it all for a shifty living as a gambler.

That too he put behind him in 1704 when he became Master of Ceremonies at Bath. There he conducted the balls and other occasions 'with a splendour never before witnessed' and it was said 'with something of the style of Louis XIV, the Sun King'.

As early as 1725, no doubt with an eye to expansion, he made the first of regular attendances at rival Tunbridge Wells' opening festivities. These were little less brilliant than his own at Bath but were 'marred by a Madman', a half-pay captain, one Drapier. One who recruited his own regiment by simply pointing a pistol at an inconsequently chosen and terrified gentleman and forcing him to sign his name on the regimental flag - in his own blood!

Nash doubtless made audible inaudible asides as to how much better all would be if he were Master of Ceremonies. It was not, however, a role he could decently seek until the death, in 1735, of that 'fine and formidable' woman Belle Causey, the 'absolute governess' of Tunbridge Wells (qv).

Under the Beau's velvet-gloved despotism, Tunbridge Wells reached its heyday. A showman to his finger tips, he dressed and lived the part. His huge post-chariot, replete with postillions and outriders and blaring French Horn was unmistakeably Nash. It was drawn by six superb greys; none of your delicately boned carriage horses but heavy farm animals which alone could haul it through rutted, pot-holed roads that became quagmires when it rained.

Liveried flunkeys would fling open the door for the Beau to emerge in matching splendour of slightly off-beat fashion, 'not quite genteel'. The ruddy, long-nosed face with its double chins (begotten perhaps of potatoes of which he was inordinately fond) was crowned with the regal white hat - so distinctive none would dare steal it. And to climax this rococo razzamataz a salvo of guns was fired to announce the arrival of the Master of Ceremonies and a new season.

Nash in his 26 years at the Wells did much to wed rumbustious frivolity with polish and politeness. Swords on the Walks and riding boots on the ballroom floor were alike forbidden. Concerts, balls, and dinners were public and well ordered, and late hour revelry frowned on. In an age of high stakes, even though his own income derived from the takings at the tables, Nash would urge sanity on reckless young blades puffed up with misplaced family pride and fortune. (The Duke of Bolton lost 8,000 guineas at a single throw at Hazard - and would have wagered 3,000 more had not Nash intervened.)

The proof of his success lay in his first season with a modern Burke's Peerage haul of '7 dukes and duchesses, 33 marquesses, earls and barons, 16 knights and 3 MPs'. Well might he have needed the latter's support for such gambling excesses were driving even tolerant Westminster to ban 'all number games'. Surprising to no one save legislators, letter-games then became the vogue: Lottery (Bingo's progenitor), Even and Odd, Rolly-Polly and Marlborough's Battles.

Beau Nash's reign ran smoothly until 1752. Then, after a fit of apoplexy, it was reported: 'He looked a-going' and an anxious versifier wrote:

'Come then Kind Health! O Quickly come away,
Beau Nash revive, and all the World be gay.'

Gradually failing in health and fortune, he lived on for nine more years, some of them in the gentle care of his mistress Juliana Papjoy, until, 87 years old, a subject under seven monarchs, he died where he had started, in Bath. There he received a kingly funeral and burial in the Abbey.

ODO, Bishop of Bayeux, Earl of Kent (1030-1097)

A Very Bad Bishop . . .

OR, TO put it more strongly, a bastard - in both meanings of the word. Pretty Arletta, the tanner's daughter at Falaise, had caught the roving eye of Robert, Duke of Normandy. So their son, Odo, became the half-brother of the equally illegitimate - and illiterate - William the Conqueror, Robert's other son.

With such a father, Odo became a youthful and wealthy bishop. And with this wealth he furnished 100 boats for his half-brother's great enterprise against England. He did much more too. For after waiting for a raging storm to abate he accompanied his men across the Channel; exhorted them on the eve of battle; and in the morning, magnificently mailed and wielding his heavy iron mace to skull-cracking effect, he led them into battle. And he did yet more when he rallied his fleeing rabble: a scene given pride of place in the 223' long Bayeux Tapestry.

Not altogether surprising for in all probability it was Odo's own brainchild created for Bayeux Cathedral which he rebuilt; for his own glorification; and to show that he, rather than William, had been the architect of a great victory at Hastings. Incidentally, it may well have been designed by an English artist and woven in a workshop at St Augustine's Abbey.

For such a great man the reward of valour was equally great: Constable of Dover Castle and Earl of Kent. That of course was only a beginning. With England firmly in his hands, William returned to his other more important realm, Normandy. So, for 15 years, Odo frequently acted as his viceroy in this country. Seizing the opportunity, it is said, he amassed 100 manors and landed estates, including Tonbridge Castle, in Kent alone. And in 12 other counties he appropriated another 100! As a Bishop, Odo showed little of his responsibilities to God for men's souls; he preferred to be custodian of military power. 'He wrought castles wide among the people, and poor folk oppressed.' His own plundering and licentious soldiery he protected but he paid scant heed to the bitter complaints of the English. And he added to his own wealth by the spoilation of abbeys and churches throughout the land.

It was in this matter that for once he met his match. When he seized lands belonging to Canterbury Cathedral, his fellow Norman, Archbishop Lanfranc, protested so strongly that the King decreed the matter should be tried on Penenden Heath, near Maidstone, for centuries the meeting place of the people of Kent when crisis threatened. After an acrimonious three-day trial, Odo was ordered to make restitution but, prevaricating, he never returned all he had stolen.

He was as ambitious as he was avaricious. In 1082 he summoned knights in his debt from all over the country to form an army. An army not for his sovereign but for himself. William returned hurriedly from

Normandy: Odo was as swiftly arrested and imprisoned. When Hildebrand, Pope Gregory VII, protested at such demeaning treatment of an honest bishop, William sent him the mail-shirt in which the warlike Odo had been captured. With it came only a quotation from the Scriptures: 'Is this thy son's shirt?'. And even on his deathbed, after a riding accident in Normandy, when he ordered the release of prisoners, Odo's name was not among them.

Release in 1087 did of course follow. With the accession of William Rufus, equally cruel, ruthless and unscrupulous, began an undercover Civil War. Odo sought to replace Rufus with William's eldest son, Robert who had been made Duke of Normandy; and then to become the power behind the throne of a weakling king. But with the capture of Rochester Castle, seized by Odo's followers, Rufus finally won the day. For Odo it was exile to the continent where, historians tell us, 'he continued to be a nuisance'.

At least until with Robert he set off on the first Crusade and died near Palermo. There he is buried in an undeservedly magnificent tomb. Was Odo fighting for his own salvation or for the booty he hoped to acquire?

PAGE, Geoffrey, D.S.O., D.F.C. and Bar, O.B.E.

One of the Few . . .

NOT Kentish born but he did two great services for the county. And therefore cannot be denied a place in this book.

He fought in the Battle of Britain - to defend Kent and England. When 56 Squadron was scrambled yet again from North Weald, it was his Hurricane that led the race to 20,000 feet to intercept over 50 'bandits'. It was his Hurricane whose fuel-tank exploded on receiving a direct hit. And it was his body which was fished out of the sea near Margate. Fished out with blistering burns to hands and face that needed two years of painful skin graft.

Not that such trifling wounds kept him grounded. Back into the air again - only to be shot down again. To be in the thick of it once more, near the end, and forced to crash land at Arnhem.

His second bonus for Kent? He was the man behind the quietly impressive Battle of Britain Memorial to the rest of the Few at Capel le Ferne. Unusual, simple, but striking, it stands on the white cliffs between Dover and Folkestone. No false heroics here. A solitary figure, a young airman, in flying kit, with arms crossed on drawn up knees, sits alone in a grass amphitheatre, the centrepiece of a huge-bladed propeller cut out of the chalk. Contemplative but ready and vigilant, he scans the skies above him.

It was in them that Page earned his honours and our undying thanks.

⁕

PETO, Sir Samuel Morton Bart, M.P. (1809-1889)

Railway Mogul . . .

MORTON (he preferred that to common or garden Samuel) started his working life as he continued it - under a full head of steam. As a builder's apprentice he not only learnt to lay 800 bricks in a day but also the skills of technical drawing. As a railway mogul, contractor and speculator in the heady era of railway mania (1840-1866) he could handle the largest and toughest gangs of roistering Irish navvies and turn them into an efficient machine.

In his early days, however, buildings were his forte. They were a rich diversity which ranged from Hungerford Market Hall to the Reform Club (1836), and from the Lyceum Theatre (1834) to Nelson's Column (1843). In later years, it was his guarantee of £50,000 towards the erection of the Crystal Palace that saved the Great Exhibition from becoming the Great Flop. But when he split from his first partner, Thomas Grissel, he lost the chance to have a hand in the re-building of the Houses of Parliament after the disastrous conflagration in 1834.

When it came to building railways, Morton was equally diverse. Not content with bringing a first line to East Anglia he turned the little seaside village into a thriving holiday resort and became known as the King of Lowestoft. Similarly it was to him that Kent owed many of its lines: Paddock Wood to Maidstone; Farringdon to Blackfriars Bridge; the London, Chatham and Dover railway (better known as the Undone, Smashem and Turnover Line after numerous accidents) that was to become his financial nightmare. The South-Eastern which brought fame and prosperity to Folkestone bears his finest memorial: the unusually long Sandling Tunnel and the towering Foord Viaduct striding magnificently across Lilliputian houses.

This was only an appetiser. Morton Peto hungered after ever wider fame. The world was to become his oyster. With Edward Betts he built the Buenos Ayres Great Southern, and the line between Blidah and Algiers where he also constructed broad boulevards - and warehouses beneath them. With Thomas Brassey, he laid lines in Canada, the Grand Trunk; in Australia; and in Europe, in France as well as Denmark.

In partnership with Broadstairs' Thomas Crampton he spread his wings yet more ambitiously - into Russia. And it was there that he and his

59

navvies laid his shortest but his most famous line, the 39 miles from Balaclava (on the Crimean Front) to Sebastopol to supply Britain's badly led and badly fed troops. For such patriotic work he would not take a penny - but in 1855 he did become Sir Morton Peto, Bart. And was to hear Gladstone describe him as 'A man with a character beyond the reach of any question'.

Railway lore is full of stories of the squalor and the sickness, of the drunkenness, violence and debauchery of the Navigators' Camps. Not so in Peto's camps. As a benevolent Baptist and Liberal he forbade the establishment of Tommy shops where work vouchers had to be exchanged for low standard food sold at exhorbitant prices. Amazingly, alcohol too was so controlled that 'gin shops were left deserted and the schoolrooms were filled'. He even provided libraries and first-aid rooms!

But for all his care, for all his drive and initiative, he over- stretched his resources in speculative ventures too eagerly undertaken without sound financial backing. Bankrupted in 1866, he sold his properties and possessions to pay his debts; to have a final fling - and to fail again.

He turned from the cut-throat competition of railway battles to retire to the tranquility of Tunbridge Wells. Twenty years later, leaving a splendid memorial in the 'Iron Horse', he was buried in in Pembury churchyard. Apparently as systematic and hardworking in private life as in business he was mourned by seven sons and seven daughters!

PETT, Phineas (1570-1647)

Master Shipwright - and Master Swindler . . .

IN A book dotted with heros and heroines, martyrs and saints, it is no bad thing to give it added tang with a sinner. Phineas Pett fits that bill to perfection.

Black in character he certainly was but not unrelievedly so. So let credit be given first - that his later misdeeds may stand out the more starkly? Undeniably he was the most skilful Master Shipwright in Kent's three important dockyards. So skilled indeed that he not only stood high in the favour of King James, 'the wisest man in Christenden', but also in the regard of Charles I who gave him a gold chain.

Phineas played no small part in the building of a still larger dockyard at Chatham - and the installation of a dry dock in 1611. The 'Sovereign of the Seas' was his and his father's pride and joy. And there were other great ships too, not only for England's navy but also for her merchant fleet, that owed their seaworthiness to him.

But there the tale of virtue ends. For, undeniably again, Phineas was a rogue. A rogue who could not resist the rich pickings that a big dockyard offered. In modern parlance he couldn't resist 'a good scam'. His impudence in this respect was so breathtaking that one can hardly resist raising one's hat to him in admiration as much as in amazement.

As we have said, Phineas built many ships for his country but, in 1604, he decided to make one for himself. Into its construction went 160 tons of the Navy's best seasoned timber. Its sails, and rigging too were 'borrowed'. And when the vessel was finally completed, still not financially satisfied, he loaded it with naval stores, guns and ammunition . . . and sailed for Spain. Not in a gallant one-man, one-ship attack, nor in a quixotic generosity for a badly mauled enemy - but to sell ship and all in it at the most handsome of profits! Admittedly, that was his highlight but for the rest, he was far from idle. Guns were sold to his admiring King's enemies; he made rich gain on private ship repairs as well as on naval so that, overstepping the mark in the repair of the 'Anne Royal', he was censored for his 'wasteful and lavish expenditure'. An artist's forgivable peccadilloes? Perhaps . . . but certainly not the buying of stores for His Majesty's ships and then re-selling them again to the Navy at no mean profit to himself. Nor was his official acceptance of stores fewer in number and value than those paid for by England's unhappy tax-payers - and the inevitable sweetener that went with the deal.

Nepotism too reigned over Chatham Dockyard. It was jobs for the boys: for Pett cousins and even half-cousins, Pett uncles and nephews - and doubtless, in a later century, it would have been Pett nieces too. His successor was of course - none other than his son, Peter. Though, let's play fair, he was as skilled a shipwright - and as fraudulent - as his father. Together, they were later accused of the 'greatest abuses'. But 'they were so knit together that the Devil himself could not discover them - unless they impeached each other'.

For all that, in 1631, Phineas, as a Commissioner and a member of the Navy Board, was chosen to escort Charles I round Chatham Dockyard where 'all sails were trimmed, rigged and at yards'. Escorted him too up the hill above the dockyard that he might see everything at a glance - and hear 'the firing of all ordnance'.

Were there no other extenuating circumstances to be found for Phineas? Well, it must be shamefacedly admitted that Sir Robert Mansel, Chief Commissioner of the Dockyard, 'totally unfitted for the job', hardly set him a shining example. When creditors pressed him, he would without hesitation dip his hands deep into the Chatham Chest - a worthy charity for underpaid seamen still further down on their luck. At every opportunity Sir Robert lined his own pocket. And, without a blush, even submitted bills to the Admiralty for work done on ships - that did not exist.

With such an example before him, can we really blame Master Shipwright Phineas Pett? Or can we . . . ?

PITT, William, The Elder; 1st Earl of Chatham (1708-1778)

The Great Commoner . . .

THE MAN who was to become Prime Minister and Viscount Chatham was born at Hayes Place, near Bromley. Amid the cares of office, its garden was his main relaxation and a small regiment of gardeners worked on it by day and sometimes even by night.

His grandfather had been the humble vicar of Blandford who shrugged off poorly paid clerical cloth to wear the richer mantle of a wealthy Indian merchant. So wealthy indeed that he was able, for £20,000, to buy a king among diamonds weighing an astonishing 410 carats. This was first bought from a native mine-worker who had smuggled it out hidden in a self-inflicted wound. So large was it that it cost some £5,000 to cut: an amount, however, offset by the sale of the resultant 'dust' and tiny chippings. It was sold at a very handsome profit to the Regent of France who set it proudly in the French Crown and later, it is said, valued it at an astronomical figure.

Chatham was a man of irreproachable character, handsome appearance and magnificent voice. After Eton and Trinity came a Cornetcy with the Blues at 23; and four years later the assumption of the family's rotten-borough at Old Sarum to become a youthful MP. Rising steadily, in 1756, he became Secretary of State. He reinforced the militia and strengthened the fleet. But it all had to be paid for. And Pitt, unflinchingly, imposed an unprecedented 10% income tax.

In that capacity, he led the country skilfully during the Seven Years War. France's armies were routed and her navies worldwide were either captured or sunk. Canada, thanks to Westerham's James Wolfe, and India, thanks to Robert Clive, became corner-stones of what was to be 'the greatest empire the world had ever seen'.

Pitt had already fallen foul of penny-pinching George II, when he supported Frederick, Prince of Wales who was petulantly demanding a larger allowance, one befitting the heir to the throne - and his expensive tastes. Pitt was caught in family cross-fire. 'Frederick is the greatest ass, the greatest liar, and the greatest beast in the whole world' stormed the

King who too had battled rancorously with his father. 'Obstinate, miserly martinet' countered his son. But at least George had been the last English king to lead his troops successfully into battle: 'Fire, and behave brave! The French will run!'

Thwarted in his ambitious plans by a king 'who would gladly give a square mile of England for an extra square yard of Hanover', Pitt was forced to resign. But because of public acclaim was reinstated within months.

In 1766, Pitt the Patriot, became Viscount Pitt, Earl of Chatham with a seat in the Lords. There he pleaded eloquently for reconciliation with the American Colonists - though not for their complete independence.

A dozen years later, deeply sunk in depression and tormented by gout, he dragged himself painfully into the House of Lords to speak on the latter issue in a voice that was a mockery of his once resonant tones. Exhausted, he sank back into his seat; rose painfully to answer a question - and fell back into the arms of his friends, a dying man.

He was accorded a public funeral; an imposing statue in Westminster Abbey - and £20,000 to pay the debts he had accumulated during his life. These, despite £10,000 left him by the Duchess of Marlborough; £3,000 per annum and a country seat by Sir William Pynsent - and of course the diamond proceeds!

PITT, William, The Younger (1759-1806)

The Churchill of his Day . . .

WITH a fascinating family background of 'Diamond' Pitt and of Pitt, the Elder, Prime Minister of England, it is hardly surprising that Pitt the Younger was precocious as a child and even more brilliant as a man.

He was born at Hayes Place, near Bromley, the home of his famous father but later lived at Holwood Park, not far from World War II Biggin Hill fighter station. In its grounds he was to give William Wilberforce his wholehearted backing for the abolition of slavery.

When only 11 he could write to his father in fittingly good Latin or Greek, and would smoke pipe for pipe with him at home. At much the same age he calmly and confidently announced: 'I wish to speak in the House of Commons.' To that end he deliberately trained and cultivated a voice whose every syllable was clear and compelling even in the longest speeches. Farmer's son and ex-Sergeant-Major, William Cobbett had an entirely different view when he referred to Pitt as 'that great snorting Bawler'.

Witty and genial, as ready to listen to others as to himself, he was never at a loss for rhetorical device or classical reference but still capable of devastating sarcasm and chilly disdain.

Eton? No! Its 'barbaric rigours' would have been too much for his frail frame so he was educated largely at home. Even Cambridge forced him back there with painful gout, despite a regularly taken prescription of 'copious draughts of port.' It was one he honoured unstintingly and without complaint all his life!

In 1780, he started to read Law at Lincoln's Inn - and in what spare time he had, haunted the Commons. In 1781, now 22, he entered it in his own right, thanks to the good offices of Cumbria's Sir James Lowther, the 'Wicked Earl' who offhandedly presented him with the seat at Appleby, just one of the nine he controlled! It was one that Pitt, hardly surprisingly, gained - but never visited. After his maiden speech, Edmund Burke, the Irish statesman and Pitt's lifelong opponent, was moved to say, 'Not a chip off the old block - but the block itself'.

Unbelievably, within two years (1783), he was Chancellor of the Exchequer. And a year later, at 24, after first having declined the post, the youngest ever Prime Minister. Although his jealous and derisive rival, Charles James Fox, predicted his downfall 'within weeks' he proved to be a little matter of 17 years out.

Few other men ever accomplished so much in so short a time. He modernised the Governments of India and Canada; achieved union with Ireland, and better relations with America (which his father had unavailingly fought for against an intransigent George III). He initiated Parliamentary reform though, with the French Revolution ablaze just across the Channel, he was to put this and *habeas corpus* on hold.

In addition, he shored up the country's crumbling finances by setting up a Sinking Fund for the National Debt; put Britain on a war footing; and united wavering European dynasties to withstand the ever-growing might of the not-so-Little Corporal.

Pitt eventually resigned, in 1801, when the King refused to approve his bill for Catholic emancipation. He was succeeded by a weak and vacillating Henry Addington, Viscount Sidmouth, only to be recalled by public acclaim:

'Pitt is to Addington
As London is to Paddington.'

Nelson's glorious victory at Trafalgar seemed to climax his policies. 'England is not to be saved by any single man' he told the world, 'She saved herself by her own exertions. And will, I trust, save Europe too by her example'. But Napoleon's dramatic victories at Ulm and Austerlitz, in 1805, were his death blow. 'Roll up that map! It will not be wanted these 10 years' he prophesied.

His ceaseless work for his country had fatally undermined his strength. Temperamentally cold, he was a dyed-in-the-wool bachelor who had never made friends readily. His last years, however, had been made less lonely by the care and devotion of his niece, Lady Hester Stanhope who had come to live with him at Walmer Castle, near Deal which went with his sinecure title of Lord Warden of the Cinque Ports. And a kindly Parliament did make a grant of £40,000 to pay his debts!

Pitt was a patriot all his life . . . to his last breath. His final words have been variously reported: 'Oh, my country! How I leave my country!' Or was it: 'How I love my country!' Was he foreseeing the perils ahead of it or simply reiterating his lifelong devotion. But surely they were not, as has been seriously reported, 'I think I can eat one of Bellamy's veal pies!' to which, admittedly, he had been vastly addicted.

PLUTO (1942-1945)

A Modern Miracle . . .

NO, not Disney's goofy dog. Not the unyielding god of the underworld, deaf to prayers and unappeased by sacrifice. Not the smallest and most distant planet (smaller than our own moon) which orbits round the sun just once every 248 years.

But the Pipe Line Under The Ocean. It helped to save tens of thousands of lives, shortened the duration of the war in Europe and, by releasing tankers, that of General Slim's beleaguered 14th Army. From a Kent point of view it stretched from Dungeness to Boulogne - a mere 25 miles. But another thousand miles of pipe stretched back to distant refineries as arteries to the heart.

Not one such arterial line but 17 were laid on the bed of the Straits of Dover! Each was made up of 40 foot lengths of pipe securely welded into one at Littlestone. Its hearts were pumping stations hidden from spying enemy planes camouflaged as tatty Dungeness holiday homes. And just in case PLUTO should hiccup, there were giant storage tanks, camouflaged too.

At the height of the war, PLUTO pumped a million gallons of the Army and the Royal Air Force's black life-blood across the Channel. By its end, its total had risen to no fewer than 172,000,000 gallons.

POCAHONTAS (1595-1617)

Jilted Princess . . . ?

CAN Death be charitably construed as a good enough reason for inclusion in this generally cheerful book? For that was the only connection between a Red Indian 'Princess' from Virginia and Kent's huddle of clapboard houses at Gravesend. As she still stands there in Kent, beautifully carved, for all to see, the author has decided that she cannot be denied.

Admittedly Walt Disney has probably now said it all. Indeed her life was so rich in romance and drama that it was the perfect scenario for a mega Hollywood 'weepie'. But in case any of my readers preferred fictional Bambi or Snow White to real life Pocahontas, here, briefly, is her story.

She was the daughter of an Algonquin Chief, Powhaton. When, in 1608, gentleman adventurer John Smith, one of Raleigh's settlers, fell into Indian hands, it was his idealistic teenage daughter, Pocahontas, who pleaded for the white invader's life rather than for his slow mutilation by the long knives of the women. Successful, she journeyed frequently to the Jamestown stockade; partly to bring provisions and information; partly too, no doubt, to see John Smith. For a 17th century teenager could be as thoroughly smitten as a 20th century one. Especially so when the object of her affection had fought under Henry IV in the Huguenot War; and against the Turks in Hungary where he was captured, imprisoned, and sold as a slave before he escaped.

John Smith, however, 'disappeared'; died, or was hidden perhaps from an importunate Indian girl who could spell 'Trouble'. And Pocahontas was shamefully held hostage for the peaceful behaviour of her warlike tribe. 'A dismal tale of betrayal and exploitation, not unusual for the English', said the cynics. In 1613, however, Pocahontas finally deserted her tribal gods for a Christian one, married John Rolfe, another settler, and exhanged exotic Pocahontas for everyday Rebecca. And, by 1616, Virginia had been exchanged for London.

There, her golden beauty dazzled Society; she took part in a Court Masque; and was actually received by Royalty. A fairy story ending? Sadly no! Homesick and scourged by the English climate, she persuaded Rolfe to take her back to Virginia. He, to his eternal credit, agreed - but perverse Fate had other ideas.

Yes, Pocahontas did indeed board a homeward-bound ship in London Docks but within a day she was forced to disembark - at Gravesend, too ill to continue. And in that alien town, she died. From fever? Consumption? Smallpox? or a broken heart? For romantic legend said that in London she had by chance seen John Smith - alive and well. Take your choice, Reader, for of this and other glimpses of her scantily recorded life story, there are a variety of different versions.

Today, Pocahontas, in Indian dress, stands tall and slim as the trees behind her, near St George's Church in Gravesend. Soil was shipped from Virginia so that the Algonquin 'princess' might sleep the more contentedly beneath it. And nearby on a plaque, Falling Sky, Two Eagles, and Little Bird on the Shoulder give the thanks of the Cherokee nation to that which 'graciously received her and treated her with great honour'.

In Virginia there is a statue of her akin to the one in Gravesend. And there are a number of well-to-do Southern families who, whilst not admitting to a single drop of Algonquin blood, proudly claim descent from her only child, a boy.

PUGIN, Augustus Welby Northmore (1812-1852)

High Priest of Gothic Revival architecture . . .

SON of a French refugee, he spent many years at Ramsgate. There he lived at The Grange, next to the windswept West Cliff. On stormy nights he kept watch from its battlemented tower for ships in distress. He had hoped to add a spire as a landmark warning of the nearby perilous Goodwin Sands but his money ran out. Generous to a degree he boarded out survivors at his own expense - and later equipped a small infirmary to care for any sick or injured.

Next door stands St Augustine's - the epitome of his Architectural beliefs. A fervent convert to Rome, in 1834, he believed that in medieval days great church architecture to the Glory of God had been achieved only by men who lived good lives. Conversely, Renaissance architecture, with its stiff symmetry and uninspired logic was 'the embodiment of Sin'. And its current advocate, James Wyatt, 'The Destroyer', was a monster of architectural depravity.

Many of the churches that Pugin designed were sited in the bleak wasteland created by the Industrial Revolution. For Pugin, only the glory of Gothic architecture could help its deprived inhabitants soar above the wretchedness in which they lived.

Much of his creed is embodied in St Augustine's church: sited, not in a drab slum, but in a sparkling Regency seaside resort. 'Rich, dark, and exquisitely over-decorated' it is an unusual delight of sculpted stone, carved wood and stained glass. In its midst he lies, robed and, in medieval style, surrounded by his kneeling children.

His best known claim to fame of course is in the still richer interior decoration of the Palace of Westminster after its disastrous conflagration in 1834. Whilst Charles Barry was responsible for the magnificent exterior, Pugin designed the equally rich interior: paintings, mosaics and stained glass as well as fittings and furniture. He died, as did Barry, before their great work was finished. (The latter's son was responsible for the completion of the top stages of the Clock Tower). Pugin, only 40, was exhausted, mentally as well as physically, from the overwork entailed by his prodigious output and his tireless devotion to the new Westminster; from financial troubles; from acrimonious dispute as to whether his or Barry's had been the finer work; from his passionate quest for perfection; and from an utterly unwarranted sense of failure.

RANSLEY, George (1782-1860)

A Man of Notoriety . . .

By day, he was a farmer's hardworking carter with an uncanny flair for handling horses; by night, a member of what John Wesley described as 'The Accursed Trade'. Physically powerful, mentally astute, he became the leader of the Aldington Blues and ruled the smuggling world from Deal to Camber.

Though born at Ruckinge, he lived most of his life at nearby Aldington Frith, a 'wild and trackless place'. In his youth he passed an honest enough life until, in 1809, he married Elizabeth Bailey, a smuggler's daughter, and a 'fine big woman' who enjoyed her gin into the bargain.

Inevitably, he was drawn into the euphemistically called Free Traders' way of life. Later, in 1821, he took part in the 'Battle of Brookland', the bloodiest of the steadily increasing number of affrays between smugglers, up to 200 strong, and the Navy's Blockade men.

The latter, from the Camber Watch Tower; harried the smugglers across Walland Marsh with volleys of shot and cutlass charges. Volleys that were wholeheartedly returned as the smugglers fled across the deep-ditched fields they knew like the back of their hands. It was indeed a running battle.

The result? Blockade: one killed and nine wounded; 'Blues': 4 killed, 12 wounded, and two captured. The only winner? Dr Hougham who not only treated the wounded of both sides impartially, but also cared for the smugglers' shot-peppered horses.

One of the prisoners was the leader, Cephas Quested. In flight, darkness and confusion he thrust his rifle into the hands of a man running pell-mell beside him, 'Here. Take this. Shoot one of the bastards.

Blow his b***** brains out'. A moment later he was looking down the barrel of that same gun - now pointed unwaveringly at him by Blockade Lt Newton, who, in a blue smock, had mingled with the fleeing smugglers.

Cephas was imprisoned and tried. Under questioning he staunchly maintained: 'I won't bring harm on others'; wrote a touching letter to his 'Dear Wife'; and was hanged in Newgate Prison. But, thanks to the intervention of a local magistrate, was spared the final indignity of his corpse hanging in chains near Brookland until his bones were picked clean.

His death was an ill wind: one that saw Ransley take over leadership of the Blues. A charismatic man, he demanded - and got - an oath of loyalty from his motley band of fishermen, ill-paid farm labourers and ex-soldiers. To charisma he added thoughtful planning.

He crossed the Channel by the Dover Packet; made shrewd purchases of brandy, tobacco, tea, lace, playing cards . . . Alerted his sea-smugglers who, in due course, would load the valuable cargo into a boat with a false bottom, and with bows and masts hollowed out. Plans laid, he would return to the Marsh in time to greet them by night on a deserted beach as they rowed in with muffled oars.

Ransley was far from alone. Anything up to 200 land-smugglers would have been marshalled into readiness with near military precision. Two thirds, the 'tubmen', to carry; a third, the 'batmen' on each flank, to protect them. And if need be to cover an orderly retreat by giving covering fire. Thus, up to 200 tubs could be swiftly spirited away by hand and horse, by pack-mule, cart or trap. Spirited away to welcoming 'hides', of which not least important were Marsh churches. Priest and rollicking versifier, R. H. Barham, swore that even on the blackest night he could find the way to his church at Snargate by the rich aroma of the tobacco stored in it!

Such runs were highly profitable. With his share, Ransley bought the 'Bourne Tap'. Like other inns it would be specially victualled for such 'Occasions'. There, it was said, 'men and women, in drink and half naked, would dance to celebrate success'. They were revels though in which Ransley, a strict teetotaller, took no part.

Such success can go to even the levelest of heads. In 1826, between May and September, seven successful runs led to an ill-planned, high-handed eighth. One onto Dover beach below the Castle casemates (today's Marine Parade): under the very eyes and noses of the Blockade. Hearing the grounding of the boats, First Rate Quartermaster Morgan and Seaman Pickett advanced without hesitation to intercept them. Morgan was shot by a long-barrelled duck-gun and was killed; Pickett was bludgeoned to the ground by their butts.

Lt Hellard, though 'a terrible man for cursing and swearing at his men', nevertheless vowed violent vengeance on their murderers. £500, no mean sum then, was straightway dangled as tempting bait. And Bow

Street runners were called in from London to question 'suspicious strangers of the lower orders.'

Within two months, the threat of the noose, or the joyous thought of £500 had worked its magic. Now names were known. The gaff was blown. Just before midnight, Lt Hellard, his Blockade men, and two Bow Street runners set off purposefully on a circuitous route to Aldington. By 3 am, in uncanny silence, the raiding party had surrounded Ransley's house; cut down his guard dog; smashed through the door; and handcuffed him (to the stoutest member of the party) before he could even scramble out of bed.

With equal speed and silence, seven other houses in the village were surrounded. The resulting 'band of ruffians' were lodged aboard the 'Ramillies' at Deal before being taken to Newgate Prison, Bow Street, and finally, Maidstone. There, before a court agog with excitement, the prisoners were sentenced to death . . . a sentence mitigated to transportation. For three months Ransley rotted in the noisome hulk 'Leviathan' in Portsmouth Harbour. There, filth, lice, fetid quarters and evil food were far more grievous than aboard the 500-ton 'Governor Ready' which, in 118 days, brought its human cargo to Tasmania - and a new life. En route, though men had been 'tiresome and larky', floggings were few - and, on deck at least, the air was fresh.

After five years of back-breaking toil, Ransley earned the customary pardon - and later, 500 acres of farmland worked, ironically, by his own gang of convict labourers. Joined by his family, he was recognised as a man of good character and some wealth. 'Respected, if not respectable' he died at River Plenty, North Norfolk.

His epitaph might well have been the words coined by George Barrington, High Constable of New South Wales - and himself an ex-con: 'True Patriot I, for it be understood, I left my country for my country's good'.

ROSE, Sir Alec (1908-1991)

Man with a Dream . . .

ROMANTIC GENEALOGISTS have come up with the idea that one of his ancestors *might* have been press-ganged into the Navy. There is, however, no doubt whatsoever that Alec Rose needed no such coercion to take to the sea - and master it.

His life began ordinarily enough in the extraordinary town of Canterbury. He followed the accepted Grammar School course to the Simon Langton School. As an extra, he sang in the St Paul's Church choir for small financial gain but great pleasure. On leaving school at 15, Alec had made scarcely a ripple on its waters. And his choice of work, first at Truscott's, the Estate Agents, and then with East Kent, the local Bus Company, held little romance. Office, however, was exchanged for open air and with it, pen for spade and plough when he ran nurseries at Littlebourne and Ash.

After some years of hard work on the land, Rose decided it was much easier to sell vegetables than grow them. And so, Central Parade, Herne Bay saw yet another shop opened, the not over-romantic 'Alec Rose; Greengrocer'.

By now he was a greengrocer who put to sea in every spare moment; one who was hooked on sailing. When he could, he sailed, mainly from Whitstable ('Its harbour then was a forest of masts, of fishing boats and yawls'). When he couldn't, he ceaselessly plotted courses across the oceans of the world. For now, the world, not Herne Bay, had become his oyster.

Like Martin Luther King, Alec Rose too 'had a dream'. It was a dream half realised when he sailed the Atlantic to win a 4th place in 'The Observer's' prestigious Trans-Atlantic Race. One such unforgettable voyage leads to another. In 1966 he made his careful preparations, said his unostentatious good-byes, and slipped off - to sail round the world! Hardly out of sight of the land he was run down in mid-Channel. Astonished friends and acquaintances joked condescendingly, 'Well that voyage didn't last long, did it, Alec?' Within the year, quite unperturbed by such a small matter and jests in such poor taste, Alec Rose and his twenty year old, 36' long ketch 'Lively Lady' set sail again to realise his dream. For greengrocer-turned-yachtsman such a voyage had to be accomplished single-handed.

For all that, he says, he was seldom lonely. In his heart he played with the laughing dolphins off the Canaries; wondered at the beauty of flying fish when he crossed the Equator (not that that prevented them being 'deliciously cooked' when in their exuberance they misjudged their flight and landed on 'Lively Lady' rather than in the Atlantic); he communed briefly with a friendly whale; chatted regularly with sun and moon; and, on occasion, confided his blind terror to the Being behind the Hand that he was quite sure took control of the wheel in moments of sickening danger.

Australia, before its Pommie-bashing days, rose magnificently to this lone Englishman. And there, not quite halfway home, he met again his son whom he hadn't seen for seven years, and the daughter-in-law and grand-children he had never known. All the more reluctantly therefore he tore himself away from the lotus land, headed South - headed for Cape Horn and the Roaring Forties.

No way did the latter let him down. 'It was a roaring hell' he remembered. Grey waves with menacing overhanging crests hissed alongside or thunderously sought to drown 'Lively Lady'. Much of the time he was navigating frighteningly blind under louring skies, sleet and numbing hail. Cape Horn itself rose, stark and terrifying, amidst a forest of jagged peaks. Howling Force 11 or 12 gales made repeated frenzied attempts to overwhelm the puny invader of their kingdom. But, in crisis, and there were many of them, there was, Alec swore, 'always that Hand on the wheel'.

More happily the Cape of Good Hope also lived up to its name. After that it was 'a holiday jaunt all the way home'. To an unwelcoming mist-shrouded Land's End. To Portsmouth where, with a proud escort of 400 yachts, Alec Rose, 58 year old greengrocer, and 20 year old 'Lively Lady' sailed in to the acclamation of a quarter of a million suddenly sail-mad patriots. He was the first Englishman ever to sail round the world single-handed - in a little matter of 353 days!

It was a feat equally enthusiastically recognised when, later, he dropped in at Buckingham Palace. And, down on his knee (for the only time) he was knighted for 'his tenacity, skill and courage'.

Alec Rose died in 1991 but years before he had written his own epitaph in best-selling 'Lively Lady'.

SHIRLEY, Doctor John, Canon Residentiary (1890-1967)

Hawkish Headmaster . . .

CANTERBURY Cathedral and King's School, Canterbury have been indissolubly wedded since the latter, the oldest Public School in England, was founded by Theodore of Tarsus towards the end of the 7th century.

Some 1200 years later, in 1935, however, it was in dire trouble. Its debts were multiplying rapidly; its numbers decreasing. Something had to be done. And that 'something' was Dr John Shirley. Having pulled Worksop College up by its boot-straps, he had seen yet another new classroom block opened - by a Prime Minister, Ramsay MacDonald before he hurried South to Kent on his rescue mission.

The future Headmaster of King's had, in 1912, been an £80 p.a. teacher; a war-serving officer in the Royal Navy; an appelant at the Bar, in 1919; and finally a Churchman: 'I could not afford to starve'.

He was a mercurial man; ruthless in achieving his goals; abrasive to colleagues; a ferocious preacher - yet able to both charm and inspire. He was a man with a clear vision of what a school could be, should be, and would be; a man with dedication and drive. He himself boasted, I'm part angel, part devil. I don't know which I shall be this week-end.'

His life was the School's - a great school beneath a great cathedral (which to sacriligious adolescents became known as Shirley's Temple). He understood boys: from the brainy to the bovine. Never taught them to a pattern but always as individuals. Could be a boy himself on Saturday afternoons as he cheered or scourged King's teams from touchline or boundary edge. Could lightheartedly dismiss an erring youngster with 'You're better be a parson: they need sinners'. And from the School as a whole he blew away the last cobwebs of outmoded tradition.

His reign (no other word for it) at King's started with a bang. He added to the School's already horrendous debts by building, not the pinch-penny Dining Hall that timorous Governors had envisaged to replace the current one that was as squalid as the dormitories, but a truly splendid one worthy of the School's long traditions and its magnificent setting in the shadow of the Cathedral. Old (and therefore expensive) war-horses were not so much led as pushed out to grass; new ones, champing at the bit, raring to go under a Headmaster obviously destined for success, foreswore current gain for future profit.

Under their drive, academic results blossomed. No League Tables then but King's, when it came to scholarships was second only to Manchester Grammar School with its vastly greater numbers. Parents were impressed. So were the rich patrons he cultivated like hothouse flowers. Newly established King's Week of the Arts even drew audiences away from Margaret Babbington's (qv) Cathedral Festival of all the talents. And who better to read the lesson in a packed Cathedral Thanksgiving Service than an Old Boy - a chap known to the World as Monty. Thanksgiving for their return from evacuation in Cornwall to buildings scarred but not shattered by the 15 bombs that fell in the Precincts.

Even before he actively set foot in Canterbury, Dr Shirley had worked for the School. Three masters and, pure gold, 22 paying boarders had been filched from Worksop. Such unblushing lack of ethics and a slightly later letter criticising his predecessor put him beyond the pale. Without hesitation the Headmasters' Conference expelled King's School. Not that Shirley cared for the opinions and longwinded conferences of other Head Teachers. He was his own man - with his own ways.

The snake in this educational Eden? A man of the cloth, the Dean of Canterbury Cathedral, the Very Reverend Hewlett Johnson. An eye-catching Red Dean at that. It was a love-hate relationship between two men of very different but equally determined principles. One that often came venomously to the boil not only at Governors' meetings but also at Chapter meetings where Shirley was never averse to stirring the Dean's already seething pot.

When retirement came after a job well done, Shirley was not so ruthlessly in a hurry. Now he had time to study yet more closely the writings of his once not far distant neighbour at Bekesbourne, the tranquil, diffident Richard Hooker. For a treatise on this gentle theologian, Oxford had already made him Doctor of Divinity.

SHOVELL, Sir Clowdisley (1650-1707)

From Powder Monkey to Admiral . . .

BORN, to poor parents, just over the Kent boundary in Hastings and probably more often at sea than in Kent. But who could be so churlish as to turn down a man with such a name - spelt in twenty-five different ways - and with such a naval record? To say nothing of a man who was elected MP for Rochester and gave that City its Guildhall clock - impressive, but strangely belittled by Dickens.

As a boy, Clowdisley is said to have swum under heavy fire, during the Dutch War, from one ship to another with dispatches between his teeth. More certainly, he tangled with Barbary Pirates who refused to release English prisoners: burnt four of their Corsair galleys and 'roughly handled' another four. He fought too at the Battle of Bantry Bay and after the defeat of the combined French and Spanish Fleets at Vigo, skilfully sailed home treasure (part of it valuable snuff) and prize-ships. In 1705, Admiral of the Blue, White and Red in turn, Sir Clowdisley was appointed Commander of the Fleet.

This was despite disaster in 1703. Even the normally safe anchorage of The Downs off Deal was not protection enough against a sudden surging storm, 'The Great Storm' that drove 16 men-o'-war and 40 merchantmen onto the Goodwin Sands, the Shyppe Swallower. Fifteen hundred sailors perished. Many more, had it not been for the skill and bravery of the local foreshore men.

Even worse disaster struck him four years later as his Squadron returned from the blockade of Toulon. At night, a howling south-westerly gale and a treacherous, ill-charted current flung 'Association', 'Eagle' and 'Romsey' too, onto The Scillies' jagged Bishop and Clerk Rocks.

Eight hundred men drowned there - but Sir Clowdisley was not among them. The waves threw his battered body onto the beach at Porthellick Cove. Not to safety but into the hands of a woman who 'extinguished his flickering life' - for the sake of an emerald ring, gleaming on his finger. It was a crime she confessed to only on her deathbed 33 years later! And the ring was then returned by the clergyman who had shrived her.

With Sir Clowdisley, drowned his two stepsons. And with their death, his wife, Elizabeth, lost to the cruel sea not only her two sons but also a second husband. Her first, another Admiral, Sir John Narborough, was a widower (whose wife had died 'mighty afflicted with a cough and big with child') who, like Clowdisley, died at sea.

There is a memorial to Sir Clowdisley and his two stepsons in the tiny chapel at Knowlton Park, near Canterbury, where he lived for a time. More ostentatiously, he is honoured in Westminster Abbey - by a tomb so thick with bas reliefs and busts that it was held to be in 'very questionable taste' - although sculpted by Grinling Gibbons.

SICKERT, Walter (1860-1942)

Multi-national Artist . . .

BORN IN Germany of Dutch and Danish parents but long resident in England! A brief career as actor taught him the art of surprise in painting as well as in drama. It was in the former that he finally made a lifelong career after studying at the Slade School of Art. Here, under Whistler, his style was moulded as it was to be when he worked with Degas in Paris. Artist, yes, but an actor all his life; the world was his theatre and the whole picture-loving public his audience.

His genres were unusually varied. He painted vibrant views of the canals of Venice; of the narrow streets of old Dieppe, of idyllic landscapes; of his much loved London music halls - their audiences as well as their artistes; formal portraits (including an unflattering one of 'My Awful Dad'); and, controversially, of low life as in 'The Camden Town Murder' and 'The Seducer'.

His best known painting is probably 'Ennui', a picture as depressing as its title: a slatternly, red-headed wife and her equally dreary husband sit, oblivious of each other, each sunk in their own apathy. 'Scenes of suburban debauchery' inveighed his critics, 'Sickert paints a world which is dirty, drab and disillusioned; a world where pleasures are mirthless; and whose devil is boredom'.

But for Sickert beauty and poetry could still be found in even the shabbiest of London lodging houses. No matter what his subject all were scrupulously drawn - then each brought to glowing life by layer upon layer of paint to achieve tonal qualities of extraordinary richness.

In 1934, when he was 74, the Depression forced him to draw in his horns, to abandon extensive London studios, and to settle at 'Hopeville' in Broadstairs. His studio however was at 10 Cecil Square in Margate. There, and at home, he painted portraits, of Edward VII and Lord

Castlerosse, and stage stars such as Peggy Ashcroft and Edith Evans - from photos! Hung them out, sometimes, on a washing line to dry. It was a Philistine practice that had his fellow artists up in arms. In between such large commissions he found time to paint in Broadstairs itself: a sunlit Baird's Hill House - and workers' cottages behind wooden palings with an abandoned bicycle sprawled on the pavement in front of them.

He also taught, conventionally, at the Thanet School of Art. Less conventionally, he stalked into the headmaster's study at one of Broadstairs many Prep Schools, Magdala Court, to demand that he teach the boys drawing at the *lowest* fee ever paid for class teaching. 'I cannot conceive Heaven' he said, 'without being able to give lessons there.'

In the town itself, he earned a reputation as a secretive, tetchy man. A youthful fellow Broadstairian, Edward Heath, sang carols outside Sickert's house. Hopefully knocked and rang. A curtain was pulled aside, a wizened, bearded face peered out. Another knock; the door jerked open as far as its chain allowed. And the future Prime Minister of the United Kingdom was told in ringing and unmistakeable terms, 'Go away, boy. Go away'.

A London acquaintance, Sir James Dunn, fared little better. Knowing times were hard, he generously commissioned half a dozen portraits. Hearing nothing of their progress he would visit Sickert at 'Hopeville' only to be peevishly asked 'How would you like it if your wife was having a baby and I came banging at your door every week to know how it was going?'.

It is surely an odd quirk of Sickert that although he delighted in painting drab and dreary London scenes, he himself was always fastidious in his person and in his choice of clothes.

SNOB

A Dog . . .

THE canine mascot of the llth Company Royal Sappers and Miners, he was annexed at Sebastopol; served in India; retired to Brompton for a well deserved life of comfort; and was buried near the Crimea Gate of the Royal Engineers, Brompton Barracks. Today, thanks to the taxidermist's skill, he still lives on in the Museum.

STANHOPE, Charles, 3rd Earl Stanhope
(1753-1816)

Man of many parts . . .

THE Stanhopes have produced many distinguished men - and certainly one distinguished woman. Charles, perhaps, was the most versatile of them all. At 15 he was obviously dedicated, like many another Kentish man, to the manly sport of cricket. In a family letter he asks for 'Twelve cricket Balls, nine inches in circumference. Five long batts, and one of these to be left-handed; and one short batt. In all six batts.' At 17 he was an accomplished silhouette profilist (the portrait photographer of his day). Numerous inventions, practical and impractical, were to become his all consuming passion.

Politics however intervened for a time. As Kent delegate in the House of Lords, soberly dressed, pale and wan, he nevertheless made his mark with a resonant voice and vigorous gesticulation. Quite unabashed, he did not hesitate to tell the Lord Chancellor that he would have to teach him Law as he had taught the Bishops religion! For his pains he was caricatured as a schoolmaster, cane in hand.

Above all, he passionately pleaded for the cessation of war with the American colonists, and for abstention from interference in Revolutionary France's internal politics. He pleaded vehemently but unsuccessfully. So vehemently indeed that he became known as 'Citizen Stanhope' and in his honour a medal was struck, derisively inscribed 'A Minority of One'! After such rejection he never attended the Lords again! However, it was doubtless some solace when the poet, W. S. Landor wrote a 20-page panegyric in which he was compared with the great Pitt - to the latter's disadvantage!

Nothing, however, stopped the flood of his inventions: fireproof stucco; a more durable cement; patents ahead of his time for steam driven vessels; an iron hand-printing press; a process of stereotyping, promptly adopted by Oxford's Clarendon Press; microscope lenses; and the building of the 200 ton 'Kent'! All of which is to say nothing of his work with Benjamin Franklyn: lightning conductors for The Pantheon in Paris!

A scientist certainly, but no architect. He disfigured Chevening, his family home, with sickly yellow mathematical tiles which limpet-like, obdurately refused later removal. However, nearly two centuries on, in World War II, the house might have fared far worse when eight bombs fell on it - but none exploded thanks to courageous Czech factory saboteurs. Today, with its lake and maze, it is the Foreign Secretary's Chequers. Obsessed with science and his inventions, sadly he had little time for his children - except when they could be used as guinea-pigs in his endless experiments. Long, ignored, they were finally heartlessly disinherited. One daughter, Hester, left her uncongenial home to live with her uncle,

Willian Pitt, at Walmer Castle; and another, Rachael, eloped with a humble Sevenoaks apothecary. In so doing she gave Gilray another opening which he eagerly seized with his jibing caricature 'The Coronet and the Clyster Pipe' (enema).

Swollen with dropsy, Charles died on Christmas Eve in 1816. And was buried among his forebears in the peerlessly beautiful Stanhope Chapel in Chevening Church.

STANHOPE, Lady Hester Lucy (1776-1839)

Society Hostess . . . Traveller . . . and Eccentric . . .

AS a daughter of Citoyen Stanhope (qv), of Chevening, it is hardly surprising that she inherited his eccentricities. Nor that with such a self-absorbed father and a mother who had time only for opera - and her own coiffeur - her education was "rambling".

But so dominant was her personality and so invincibly cheerful her nature that, within the family, she caught the shrewd eye of Uncle William, William Pitt the Younger, Prime Minister of Great Britain. In 1803 she left her uncongenial home and lived with him at Walmer Castle as 'an aristocratic ornament of drawing-rooms and the confidante of statesmen'. Versatile, she also planted flowers and clipped yews in the dry moat of the Castle, The Dell. (From it she may well have witnessed the 'Yankee Robert Fulton demonstrating his recent inventions of submarine and torpedoes that Napoleon had already turned down.) Not unnaturally, Pitt overlooked her 'dazzling indiscretions' (which included once blacking his face with cork): 'I let her do as she pleases; for if she were resolved to cheat the Devil she could do it!'.

His death in 1806, after devotedly nursing him in illness, was a sickening blow. Two others followed in shattering succession at Corunna, her brother and General Sir John More, for whom she had had the warmest affection, were both killed: the latter in the hour of victory after an epic retreat. It was too much. And in 1810, with a £1200 pension from the King, her faithful companion, Miss Williams, her doctor who was to become her admiring Boswell, and a suitably impressive entourage, she left England - never to return.

Undaunted by shipwreck off Rhodes, she made a stately pilgrimage into Jerusalem. Then headed for the Levant to a decaying castle at Djoun, high on the slopes of Mount Lebanon, which she turned into a refuge for the sick and homeless. There she also intrigued joyously and tirelessly; and even 'waged war' on both the Egyptian Viceroy and a succession of British Consuls whom she regarded and treated with aristocratic contempt.

Now an egocentric virago and self-styled Queen of Arabia, she ruled over nearby Druse villagers equally despotically but with an open-handed generosity that was to bankrupt her. She found no small solace in her ever increasing army of cats, and in her horses which she superannuated in strict order of seniority.

Thirty attendants, even for an Oriental Queen and Holy Prophetess, seemed to be overdoing it. Even so she complained bitterly that she was neglected. Syrians, though 'thievish and dirty', she found made the best servants for they were obsequious and could be trained 'neither to smile nor scratch themselves' when they waited at table. More, they had no fancy 'Union' ideas as to hours of work; or even as to be legality or illegality of being beaten with strong language or a stout mace. After all, they knew that with her there were rich pickings for the taking.

Of her, Lytton Strachey wrote, 'Lady Hester's nose was a nose of wild ambition, of pride grown fantastical; a nose that scorned the Earth, it was a nose altogether in the air.'

Despite her alleged isolation she received a steady stream of distinguished visitors. These she would harangue for hours on a wide variety of topics, ranging from the virtues of concubinage to anecdotes of her life with Pitt. One young man, forced to stand in The Presence, fainted after a non-stop two-hour flow.

Visitors became fewer; the depredations of her servants more frequent. In 1838 she walled herself in her castle, managed to borrow enough, even from wily Levantines, to pay her ever-increasing debts . . . Then, in 1839, in proud isolation 'a feeble, impoverished, pipe-smoking emaciated wreck', she died. Her servants, human vultures, straightaway decamped with everything of value. She herself was buried in her own garden at night, by torchlight.

STUART, Frances (1648-1702)

Britannia Triumphant . . .

SHORTLY after the hideous ravages of the Great Plague (5,000 dead in a week with sick and healthy alike barricaded into their own homes - to live or to die) Charles II was in another quandary. Voluptuous My Lady Castlemaine, favourite among his many mistresses, had rather publicly presented him with a son on Christmas Day from the scholarly atmosphere of Merton College. But his Portuguese-born queen, Catherine, regrettably seemed incapable of following her good example.

And now, drat me, there was this new Maid of Honour, this La Belle Stuart, as she had become known. With whom, Pepys had 'fancied myself sporting with her with great pleasure'.

Charles was being rapidly driven to distraction, not merely by her lithe figure and long legs, not merely by her happy vivacity, but by her tenacious virtue. Admittedly her dissipations were nothing more than hunt the slipper, slightly indecorous Blind Man's Buff . . . and building towering but ephemeral card houses! It was her very innocence, and a certain French flair, that kept Charles in hot pursuit. And yet . . . this determined virgin unblushingly recounted to the Court how that very night she had dreamt that she slept with three ambassadors!

La Belle Stuart did succumb to her Sovereign's advances - just once. Then, rather lightly clad, helmeted, and spear in hand, she posed for Rossellier - and is happily still with us on our coinage as Britannia!

However she could not bear Charles' constant pursuit so, one winter's night, muffled in her cloak, she slipped out of Whitehall and headed for the 'Beare' at Southwark, the arms of the Duke of Richmond (whose wife had died only a fortnight previously), his coach, Cobham Hall - comfortable in its red brick serenity - and marriage.

Charles was not so much furious as deeply pained, grievously hurt. That the one on whom he had lavished such tender care and brotherly affection should betray him! And when, only a year later, poor Frances was scourged by smallpox he had the grace to let it be known - indirectly of course - that he prayed it would spare her face. And so (virtue rewarded?) it did.

Her unmarred portrait for many years hung in the Long Gallery. Presumably, now that the Hall is a girls' public school, the painting has been removed to safer quarters. But what a splendid example she would have been to England's young and yearning womanhood.

DR SYN

Purely fictional . . .

BUT too redolent of Kentish romance to be omitted. Born belatedly at Dymchurch, in 1915, of author Russel Thorndike, actress Sybil Thorndike's brother. An 18th century Jekyll and Hyde: one day the respected village parson; the next, the vicious pirate and smuggler, Cap'n Clegg alias The Scarecrow. One day smoking a pipeful of Virginia tobacco and drinking a hot toddy of smuggled brandy in a low seafarer's inn; the next, penning long and pious sermons in his study.

George Arliss brought him to life on the screen in 1937. Thorndike returned to him with a handful of popular sequels, and, in 1962, Cap'n

Clegg was portrayed by Whitstable's Peter Cushing (qv), Hammer House of Horror's ever ready Frankenstein.

NOT to be confused with Rowlandson's caricature of a simple minded clergyman, Dr Syntax! The latter on his ancient nag, Grizzle, sought, despite misadventure after misadventure, to write a Guide Book on The Lake District. A gentle jab at Wordsworth and Co.

❦

THORNDIKE, Dame Sybil, Companion of Honour (1882-1976)

A Star of Life - as well as of Stage . . .

SHAW and Shakespeare, Greek Tragedy and Grand Guignol were her strengths. Remarkably, in Sybil Thorndike and Ellen Terry, Kent boasted two of Britain's finest 20th century actresses.

At four she was acting parlour-pieces at her home in Minor Canons' Row in Rochester. Three years later she was co-director, author and star with her brother Russell in 'The Dentists' Cure' (or 'Saw Their Silly Heads Off'). In her teens she switched her bounding enthusiasm to the piano but practised with such determined ferocity that she developed chronic pianist's cramp . . . The Concert Hall's loss was undoubtedly the Stage's gain.

Her life and education continued in Dickens' Rochester, and then at the Slade School of Art in London. On the morning of a vital stage interview with Charles Wyndham, she was mysteriously struck down with sickness. Her father, now vicar of Aylesford Church, Kent's 'third Cathedral', piously thanked God for saving his daughter from a life of stage sin. The Deity however did not intervene a second time - and Sybil was signed on, in 1904, with Ben Greet's Touring Shakespearean Theatre, booked for America.

With Sybil went her much less experienced brother Russell. This, largely thanks to her loyal and unblushing lies. 'Those eyes! They can make your blood run cold.' In an exacting tour that left no theatre unturned in the length and breadth of that vast country, she played no fewer than 112 different parts! Many of them as understudy for lead actresses laid low by the gruelling schedule and seemingly endless jolting journeys. And witnessed a murder below the windows of her sleazy, downtown hotel! On her return to England she joined the Repertory Company run by Miss Frederica Horniman, the daughter of a wealthy Quaker tea- merchant, in Manchester's Gaiety Theatre. There, in Shakespeare, in Greek tragedy, and in modern plays she gradually took leading roles. Of those by far the most important and idyllically happy one, however, was as the wife of her Director, Lewis Casson. And when she was 80, and he 90 they were still together - celebrating their Diamond Wedding.

In 1907, she played in a farce, 'The Marquis', and had the great good fortune to have G.B.S. seated in the front row. Impressed, he offered her a part in 'Widowers' Houses'. The seed had been sown. Some years later he saw her with new eyes. 'I have found my Joan!' he triumphantly told his wife. And in 1924, Sybil, tall, strong of face, and commanding, held the world of theatre spellbound with 244 sterling performances in the title role. 'That was my peak' she claimed.

Back in 1914, Lilian Bayliss had invited her to join the Old Vic. Lydia Languish and Lady Teazle followed Portia and Ophelia. Post War it was a two-year Grand Guignol stint at The Little Theatre - with both her husband and her brother joining in the ghoulish fun. That is, if you could call 'Hound of Death'; 'Kill and Fear'; and 'The Old Ladies', in which Sybil had her eyes gouged out by knitting needles, fun?

In 1944, after touring the Welsh mining valleys, her career soared on to its zenith: the Old Vic with Ralph Richardson and John Gielgud; the National Theatre with Laurence Olivier in 'Uncle Vanya'. A rich life indeed!

Gently downwards then as new stars shone more brightly in the theatrical sky. Her career had spanned over 50 years. At 70, she could laugh off a flop - Thackeray's monumental 'Vanity Fair' as a musical! 'What is life for,' she asked wryly, 'if nothing is ever ventured?'.

At 77, she made her final stage appearance, in the comedy thriller 'Arsenic and Old Lace'. Belatedly, a year later, came the Companion of Honour. 'She was the most loved actress since Ellen Terry' said John Gielgud.

'I want Bach's Toccata and Fugue played at my funeral. If it isn't, I shall jolly well want to know why!' typified her forthright character.

THORNTON, Charles Inglis (1850-1929)

Swashbuckling Cricketer . . .

EDUCATED at Eton. Here he shone at such diverse sports as the Wall Game, Fives, Throwing the Cricket Ball, Racquets, Putting the Weight . . . And he hardly endeared himself to the county he was to adopt in 1867 when he took all 10 of Canterbury's King's School's wickets - with sneakers! On to Trinity College - and to steer Cambridge home on three occasions out of four against Oxford.

He hit cricket balls even more prodigious distances than he threw them. His best effort of 169 yards was marked and verified by a trustworthy man of the cloth, vicar and cricketer the Rev James Pycroft. He had nearly been brained by it as he entered the Hove ground!

Other match-play incidents were hits impartially over the old pavilion at Lords and at the Oval; nine sixes out of Tunbridge Wells ground in a single innings; and a six off each of the four balls of an over at Canterbury's St Lawrence Ground. To say nothing of a well struck blow that sent an inoffensive ball over a four storey house into Trafalgar Square - not in London, but in Scarborough where he did so much for their famous Festival.

Placement, as well as power, was one of his cricketing virtues. On one occasion he hit a ball twice through the same window of a neighbouring house. Hopefully not after it had been repaired!

Mark you, he had considerably more freedom of movement than the modern cricketers encumbered by all today's battle armour from top of head to tip of toe, leaving little of the human frame vulnerable. Pads? Never! Gloves? Well, just one, descended to only late in his career. But then he did not have to face the demonic 6 ft 7 in of Curtly Ambrose or Courtney Walsh, did he?

Charles enjoyed action off pitch as well as on. And undoubtedly found it when he coolly travelled through Japan . . . Russia . . . and Siberia. Rather more prosaically he was an avid filmgoer. And in a bulging wallet he carried with him newspaper cuttings of the most unsavoury murders in the previous 25 years.

Nor was he short of youthful low cunning. When calling to the toss of a Victorian coin, he would belatedly call 'Woman'. And was, of course, invariably right! Once, at Oakham, to 'Do you play cricket, Sir? We're a man short' he taciturnly replied that he had done - a bit. And, without so much as a blush, rang up 188 out of 216 in two hours, hitting the ball out of the ground 13 times.

Charles was a man of determination and, occasionally, of patience. 'I told you I'd do it eventually, Jim' he said to the Surrey spinner Southerton after he had at last hit him out of the Oval. Unperturbed, Southerton replied, 'I'll get you, Mr Thornton. I'll get you.' And he did.

A member of the M.C.C. for 50 years, Thornton died suddenly in 1929, aged 79.

TULLIS, Julie

Mountaineer of Character . . .

FROM High Rocks Inn and Harrison Rocks to the High Himalayas is a little matter of 15,000 feet and 10,000 miles. It was a transformation that Julie took in her stride. She ran patient classes for the handicapped and deprived at the former; climbed enthusiastically and expertly whenever opportunity presented on the latter or the Alps.

Went one better when she was selected for an assault on K2, second only to Everest. Step by step she fought Nature at its toughest. Fought it alongside the finest male mountaineers in the country. And, trapped by a ceaseless and unrelenting blizzard, died with them.

TYLER, Wat (Died 1381)

Demagogue and Rebel . . .

KNOWN by his trade Wat had most certainly been a mercenary in the French Wars. And on his return had put his military expertise to good use as a part-time highwayman. It was his fiery temper and his tiler's hammer which were the sparks that set the Peasants' Revolt in 1381 blazing into near Civil War.

The Poll Tax was as hated then as in the 1990's. Hated by Tyler still more when a lecherous tax collector 'in a most unmannerly way' sought to prove his daughter's womanhood, and therefore her eligibility to pay the tax. Outraged, Tyler used his hammer with telling effort.

Dartford - and Kent - rose as one man to his dynamism in what they saw as a blow against an iniquitous tax, against their poverty-stricken lives of virtual serfdom, and of their liability to be branded on the forehead if they dared demand an increase in their starvation wages. 'London . . .' was the cry. 'Down with all traitors.' All they wanted was to root out and destroy the corrupt officials who they firmly believed had led astray their youthful king, Richard II, son of the Black Prince and the Fair Maid of Kent.

First, however, Tyler led his followers to Maidstone to rescue John Ball, a hedge-row preacher from the dark dungeons of the Archbishop's riverside Palace. Ball became the spiritual leader, Tyler the miliary one, of the ever-swelling tide of simple villagers 20,000 strong but armed only with pitchfork, flail or cudgel. Then to Canterbury where the mob stormed its tumultuous way into the Cathedral during High Mass to demand the death of the traitor, Archbishop Sudbury. For good measure they stormed the Castle to destroy records and free luckless prisoners.

Having marched 80 miles in two days Tyler, with others from a dozen Southern counties, encampted his force below two swirling banners of St George on Blackheath. There under his leadership they sacked the Archbishop's Palace; freed the scum of London from the Fleet Prison and from the Marshalsea, pausing at the latter only long enough to torture its Keeper who himself had 'tortured without pity'.

Aldgate and Billingsgate were flung open to the rebels by the London mob. Irresistably the tide swept on to sack John o' Gaunt's Savoy Palace of the finery he himself had pillaged in France - and then to fire it. On swept the ill-armed rabble to seize the 'impregnable' Tower of London itself when the portcullis was indecisively raised to await the King's return to his bolt-hole. From its Chapel, Archbishop Sudbury and the Treasurer, Sir Robert Hales, 'Hob the Robber', were dragged from their prayers to Tower Hill. There to be summarily and crudely beheaded across a log of wood.

The former's head with once proudly worn mitre set askew on it, was paraded through the streets. Streets where rows of wooden houses were set alight by blazing torches; and old scores were bloodily settled as, drunk on huge barrels of free ale, 20,000 men ransacked and raped. Terrified courtiers hustled Richard into Baynard's Castle to escape the slaughter.

But next day the 14 year old youth, handsome and slender, accustomed to 'robes stiff with jewels', knelt in solemn prayer in Westminster Abbey. Then calmly rode to Smithfields to face Tyler and his poverty stricken followers already half appeased by hastily given promises of less crippling taxes and the restitution of their ancient rights.

Tyler, drunk with power, and incensed by the Keeper of Rochester Castle's charge 'Thou art the greatest thief and robber in the county of Kent' was haughtily insolent. And, dagger in hand, behaved in 'very rude and disgusting fashion'. Much affronted, William Walworth, Mayor of London, reproved him scathingly: 'How dare you address your Sovereign thus'. Infuriated, Tyler struck out with his dagger only to hear it clash futilely on armour . . . and to feel the Mayor's sword across his head and neck. As Tyler lay bloodily sprawled from his horse, Richard with a shrewdness beyond his years seized his chance.

'I am your Captain. I will be your leader. Let him who loves me follow me.' And even as their leader, on Walworth's orders, was dragged out of St Bartholomew's Hospital and stabbed, follow him they did. As they swarmed peacefully around him, he reasoned with them and offered them free pardons. Even with loyal troops now about him, Richard refused to take bloody reprisals.

The revolt, for which Tyler had given his life, died too. But within a decade the young darling of the Kentish rebels had become a still greater despot. But one who was himself to die in Pontefract Castle's dungeons, hungrier than any Kentish villager had ever been - deliberately starved to death.

WEBB, Captain Matthew (1848-1883)

First across the Channel . . .

JUST because a man is born in a county, Shropshire, that does not boast Kent's magnificent coastline, is no reason to preclude him from this book. Especially when, emulating Julius Caesar, he came to Kent, saw, and conquered the Straits of Dover.

He was one of a Wellington doctor's well-assorted children: 8 boys and 4 girls. When he was only 8 he bravely rescued a younger brother from drowning. It was a feat that he vainly attempted again years later. Then, as 2nd Mate of Cunard's 'Russia', travelling at 15 knots, he dived into the sea to save a sailor who had fallen from high up in the rigging. For this dangerous attempt he was awarded the first Stanhope Medal. As free with his money as with his life, he gave the £100 raised by cheering passengers to his mother.

As a youngster he had strolled nonchalantly, hands in pockets, across the narrow parapet of Buildwas Bridge, high above the river; and in friendly contest outlasted a brash Labrador's challenge by out-swimming him over 90 minutes. When he was 12 he joined the tall-ship 'Conway', a mercantile training school. So well had he learnt his sea-lessons that only 15 years later he was the thrusting Master of the sail-and-steam-powered 'Emerald'.

Oddly, within months he had resigned and had begun training for the new venture which was to bring him much fame but little fortune. Part of his routine preparation was to swim from Westminster Bridge to Regent's Canal Docks; from Blackwall Pier to Gravesend; from Dover to the Varne buoy; and even from Dover, past Caesar's landing place at Deal and Archbishop Becket's at Sandwich, to Ramsgate.

By 12th August 1875 he was ready - but the sea wasn't. After six hours heartbreaking struggle through driving rain and seas so rough that even hardened Pressmen in the pilot's accompanying lugger were seasick, just before midnight he wisely admitted defeat, although he had covered nearly half the distance. It was however only a temporary defeat. On the 24th, wearing not the unspeakable reach-me-down costume of his day but scarlet bathing trunks as well as several layers of porpoise oil Webb again plunged into the sea from Dover's Admiralty Pier. At an unyielding 20 powerful breast strokes a minute, he drove on through more accommodating waves towards Calais. Hours later, however, contrary winds and tides swept him off course: for over an hour he swam but made no headway at all. Once he was stung by a starfish; once entangled in sea-weed. Angry but unperturbed he plugged tirelessly on with little sustenance except beef tea laced with brandy or cod liver oil.

So, Webb had to endure a second night of darkness and disorientation of monotony and mental strain. But at 10.40 am he trumphantly stood up on Calais sands just West of the harbour. Blanketted, and bundled into a trap he was driven through crowds of cheering Frenchmen to the Hotel de Paris. There 'bright as a bird' but no thanks to a band hurriedly hired to lull him 'to slumbers', he slept for 15 hours. In 24 hours 45 minutes non-stop swimming, wind and tide buffetted, he had covered, not 22 direct miles but roundabout 39½! No man deserved his sleep more!

Next day he cheerfully rejected the 50 francs fee demanded by a local doctor who had merely made a hurried examination of tongue and pulse. 'After all', he told the excited medico, 'only in trunks I hadn't much chance of carrying a purse. Still, I'll pay you next time when I drop in for another little swim'. And then back to Dover - this time by ferry.

There, the 24th Regiment gave him its '24 honours' and a Burmese Silver Cup. At the Royal Cinque Ports Y.C., it was the Mayor of Dover's turn to praise him: 'The nation will be proud of you. Yours is a feat that may never be repeated'. At Wellington, excited townsfolk unhitched his horses and proudly pulled his carriage themselves. Ahead of him was a detachment of the 6th Shropshire Rifle Corps, and ahead of them the Band of the 7th Shropshires blaring out 'Here the Conquering Hero Comes'. At nearby Ironbridge, Webb himself wrote, 'I am being nearly eaten alive by the proud Salopians'. And in London, at the Stock Exchange, before 1500 clamorous people, he received a cheque for £1400 - £500 of it straightaway given to his father!

Acclaim wherever he went. But no worthwhile post or financial backing for his inventions of an ingenious bicycle; a swimming machine; and a screw-propeller. There was nothing for it but an aquatic circus. And what greater boost could he give it than to swim through the rapids and whirlpools below Niagara Falls? Not even Webb's iron muscles and iron determination could overcome that near-suicidal challenge. This time the 'impossible' became the 'insurmountable'!

* * * * *

Dover's Mayor was either over-elated or under-educated in the rapid progress of science when he ventured 'It may never be repeated'. Indeed it was nearly 60 years before Edward Temme, a British Olympic Water Polo player (who had already swum the Channel in the reverse direction in 1927) followed in Webb's strokes - and in some 15½ hours.

With the advent of a more scientific approach, time steadily diminished until in 1973 when 16 year old Lynne Cox swam it triumphantly in only 9.65 hours. Within a fortnight the record was snatched from her by an ungallant American, Richard Hart. Equally ungallant, she snatched it back within a year. In 1983 it was a 12 year old, Samantha Druce, who swam the Channel from Cap Gris Nez to Dover in 15 ½ hours.

Australian Clifford Batt swam it when he was 68. And Jabez Wolffe with a grit equal to Webb's, made 20 attempts - all unsuccessful! The last when he was only yards from the shore. And in 1981 Jan Erikson, U.S.A. surely achieved the ultimate: a triple crossing in 38½ hours.

A nine-hour crossing may sound easy compared with Webb's but the words engraved on his profiled plaque in his home town 'Nothing Great is Easy' still speak the truth. And even in death Webb had achieved 'a vast ocean of good' by giving a great boost to swimming and its organised development. Today, a bronze bust of Matthew Webb still looks out from Dover promenade across the Channel he was the first to conquer.

WELLINGTON, Arthur Wellesley, 1st Duke of Wellington (1769-1852)

Lord Warden of the Cinque Ports . . .

LIKE that other 'Saviour of England', Lord Kitchener, he was an Irishman, born Wellesley, not Wellington. (To avoid confusion, the latter title, though not awarded until 1814, is used throughout.)

His education at Chelsea . . . Eton . . . Brussels . . . and Angers might well be classed as 'peripetetic'. So too might his army postings: 7th Foot to 41st Foot, 41st to 12th Light Dragoons, on to the 58th Foot and finally, with a commission purchased for him by his brother, to the 33rd Foot.

His father was an improvident Anglo-Irish peer. By him Arthur was regarded as the dullard of the family - and the army as the last refuge for well-born idiots. As a young officer Wellington spent years of social trivialities, gambling and debauchery in Dublin as aide de camp to the Lord Lieutenant. In a brief spell of action in Holland in 1794 the unnecessary suffering and loss of life not only made a lifetime's mark but also determined him to make his way in the Army.

This he did when he was posted to India, in 1797, under the command of another famous Kentish man, General George Harris. Thus, for once, he beat his already distinguished brother, Richard, to it by a short head when the latter arrived some months later to become Governor-General no less. There Wellington helped to crush the ambitious and rebellious Tippo Sahib, Sultan of Mysore. And there, by now an acting Major-General with 7,000 men of whom only 800 were English, he put to rout 40,000 Mahrattas.

After these successes followed others. He won over the electorate of Rye to become their M.P. And, vastly more important, he was now considered well enough established to marry his long cherished, but muddle-headed Kitty Pakenham, 'of the dancing eyes'. A brief honeymoon, then, perhaps a shade too eagerly, Wellington sailed to

Portugal for greater, if less pleasurable conquests. But had he really gained the day with Kitty? For later she was, unblushingly to admit that she had sent him not one single love letter during his absence.

In Portugal he drove out the French in a series of brilliant campaigns only for his political masters to agree a far too lenient Convention of Cintra. Public opinion was outraged: Nature-loving William Wordsworth was moved to words of wrath: 'The British Lion has become a beast of burthen'; and Byron to write:

'Pens, tongues, feet, hands combined in wild uproar;
Mayors, Aldermen laid down the uplifted fork;
The Bench of Bishops half forgot to snore;
Stern Cobbett who for one whole week forbore
To question aught . . . '

Wellington, the conquering hero, did escape the worst of the opprobium though 'For a time I did not know whether I was to be hanged, drawn and quartered, or roasted alive.'

His continuing campaigns in Spain and France culminating in his supreme victory at Waterloo are too well known to bear repeating. He achieved his great successes by a rigidly imposed self-discipline; an ability to make the most of the slenderest means; to command indefatigably from the saddle; to turn his 'scum of the earth' into 'such fine fellows'. Often reserved and tense, he would on occasion erupt into volcanic laughter . . . or terrifying rage.

From then on, although he was Commander-in-Chief for the rest of his life (volunteering for active service when he was over 70) he became politician and Premier as well as a revered father figure for the nation. Honours were attracted to him as iron filings are to a magnet: to his rank of Field Marshal (1813) and his title of Duke (1814) were added Master of the Ordnance, Constable of the Tower, Constable of England. And, on his retirement in 1828, Lord Warden of the Cinque Ports, Constable of Dover Castle and Admiral of the Cinque Ports for life. With this sinecure went Walmer Castle: one of Henry VIII's three squat, 'English Rose' concentric forts built near Deal to give maximum fire-power and minimum target area should the French seek to invade.

'It is the most charming sea-residence I have ever seen' he boasted. And, rather unwisely, added, 'Even the Queen herself has nothing to compare with it'. Upon which that Lady invited herself to Walmer, not for a weekend but for three weeks! The Duke transferred to the Ship Inn whilst his own simple soldier's quarters were torn to pieces to provide more fitting royal accommodation for his monarch. Unperturbed he growled, 'It don't signify. I'll soon knock it all back again'.

Pitt's room became Royal Dining Room; Wellington's laundry, after the mangle had been given its marching orders, became the guardroom. All went well enough with the Royal couple touring the surrounding countryside by day and decorously reading Hallam's 'Constitutional History' by night. All that is, except that despite (or was it because of it?) 13' thick walls with deep splayed windows it was a little draughty. And as a result the Queen Empress did suffer a cold.

Apart from such a visit, and one by a Russian Grand Duchess, Wellington lived much in his own room looking out to sea: sparsely furnished with compact writing desk, camp-bed with his silk-covered campaign mattress, a camp-chair that had seen long service, and Blucher's velvet blanket.

At 6 o'clock he rose to walk the battlements. Having breakfasted, his day followed a fairly regular pattern. A ride or a jaunt in his pair-horse blue phaeton (which he drove unconventionally from the left in order that his companion might have the necessary benefit of his good ear) to Dover Castle, to which he had to give the password or countersign.

For the rest it was largely a matter of writing letters; talking with friends; reading 'The Standard'; a late evening gossip under his favourite lime tree, or a little, a very little work in the now overgrown garden that Lady Hester Stanhope had created for Pitt. For that he had some sporadic help from an old soldier who grumbled, 'Ah know nowt about gardening'. Unperturbed, as he had always been under enemy fire, Wellington counter-attacked with 'No more do I! But we can learn'. And of course there were always his not-too-arduous official duties as Lord Warden, such as processing to deal out justice at his age old Warden's Court.

He delighted too in the company of old friends such as Arbuthnot of the Treasury (with whose handsome wife he was long in platonic love) and Croker (a fellow MP much concerned with Ireland). An expedition to visit the latter did the master military strategist no credit at all. Dover to Folkestone by train went as planned. But the alleged half-mile walk to Croker's house turned out to be three - mostly uphill at that. For once the victor of Waterloo turned tail to seek a reinforcing gig in Dover - but first to learn that Croker was not at home - but actually visiting Dover!

If the Iron Duke turned tail at Folkestone he was often on his knees at Walmer. Breakfast over, he was subject to attack by half a dozen small skirmishers: his grandchildren who came to bid 'Dukey' Good Morning. Long arms quickly encircled them, three to an arm - and if one laughing little girl escaped she heard the cry 'I'll get ye! I'll get ye!'.

In September 1852 he gave the customary order for his carriage to be ready for a journey to Dover. Then suddenly sank back again into his high-backed chair. And shortly after, died.

For many years Walmer Castle, outranking even London's grandiose Apsley House or Hampshire's rural Stratfield Saye, had been his favourite retreat. So it was not unfitting that the man who had saved Europe should die there amid Kent's tranquility.

WILLES, John (1777-1852)

Innovative 19th century cricketer . . .

IN 1807, not long after the fall of the Bastille, he revolutionised cricket. Instead of bowling conventionally underarm, he bowled - to the shock and horror of the cricketing world - ROUND ARM! It was an action that wreaked havoc among the stumps; that raised howls of protest, every scrap as loud as those to come against bodyline in Australia, or against the bumping barrage of West Indian giants.

Worse still it was an action taught him by a mere chit of a girl - his sister! When he was in need of practice he dragooned her into action in a barn at his Tonford (Canterbury) home as a bowler, and his dog as a tireless out-fielder. As fashionable skirts grew ever more voluminous, so her action, of necessity, grew ever higher and ever more effective. And cricket pundits averred: 'John Willes, his sister and his dog could beat any Eleven in England.'

Brother John latched onto the idea smartly - with great success. Until, in 1822 at cricket's Mecca, Lords, he was no-balled. Threw down the ball, and rode not only out of Lords - but out of the game too for ever. Already the best shot and boxer in Kent, he found some solace in hunting - with his own pack.

WOLFE, James (1727-1759)

Victor in war; vanquished in love . . .

The man who was to drive the French out of Canada was born in the peaceful vicarage of the equally peaceful village of Westerham, near Sevenoaks. He was born of a mother who claimed descent, perhaps a little optimistically, from Edward III and the warlike Hotspurs; and of a father, 20 years older than his wife, who was a Lieutenant-General of the 8th Regiment of Foot. After the birth, mother, child, and father now back from active service, returned to their imposing tall and gabled home, 'Spiers'. (Now the National Trust Quebec House Wolfe Museum).

Hardly surprising, therefore, that James' career was a military one. One in which he had already achieved brilliant success at a time when lesser mortals were just beginning to learn their trade. Not that attending Swinden's Academy at 11, when they moved to Greenwich, ranked highly though there he did make friends with one, plain Jack Jarvis - later to become Admiral the Lord St Vincent: three times to relieve Gibraltar and once to crush a Spanish fleet twice the size of his own off what is now known in his honour as Cape St Vincent.

Even in those precocious days it was not common for a 14 year old to be commissioned. Let alone to carry the colours when reviewed on Blackheath. Only two years later James saw much livelier action, with the 12th Regiment of Foot at Dettingen (1743). (The last time an English monarch was in action with his troops). In the centre of the first line they suffered the heaviest of casualties - and his horse was shot from under him. Bitterly he complained that for the two following days he had to carry out his adjutant's duties on foot - and in heavy riding boots!

He missed most of Butcher Cumberland's slaughter of hungry and ill-armed Scots at Culloden (1746) but when ordered to shoot a wounded prisoner refused the command point-blank: 'My Commission is at your Royal Highness's disposal'. Eight years of enervating garrison duty followed during which he felt it necessary to acquire the social graces of Latin, Literature - and Dancing! Chafing at the bit for action, however, he fumed, 'The country is fast going upon its ruin with its paltry projects . . . and with the ridiculous actions of those to whom they are entrusted'.

In 1757, action eventually came at Rochefort on the French Atlantic coast. There he showed reckless bravery and initiative in an attack sadly bungled by his superiors. Fearlessly, if tactlessly, he told the world: 'We blundered most egregiously on both sea and land.' And, by court martial, the Commander, Sir John Mordaunt, paid for it. A furious George III stormed at his advisers: 'Mad, is he? Then I wish to God he would bite some of my other Generals'.

The only campaign in which Wolfe failed was his courtship of Cumbrian Elizabeth Lawson. The siege lasted four arduous years but was lost through constant enemy sniping - sniping by his mother: 'She has altogether too small a fortune'. Elizabeth was to remain a spinster, and he, though he reputedly had as good an eye for a pretty girl as for an enemy weakness, a bachelor. It was said that even years afterwards he still could not bear to look upon her portrait. (Take that as you will!)

'Wolfe is to War as Pitt is to Politics' became the people's cry. And Pitt, as shrewd as ever, had had his eye on him as the very man for his grandiose plan to drive the last French out of Canada.

So, in 1758, with Major-General Amherst (another Kentish man) he landed on Cape Breton Island and laid siege to Louisbourg, the Gateway to the St Lawrence . . . to Quebec. As an unexpected bonus he found 'The Americans (Canadians?) are the most cowardly contemptible dogs . . . they desert by battalions'. But, not unwillingly, they joined his forces. Thus reinforced, Wolfe, with 'Merit, great spirit and alacrity', led his men over shockingly rocky terrain to storm and take the fortress itself.

A year later he was back: now a Major General and in full command of the operation. Only to be attacked, not by the French, but by his old enemies of debilitating gravel and tuberculosis. He turned to his surgeon. 'I know you cannot cure my complaint. But pray make me up so that I may be free of pain for a time and able to do my duty'.

Quebec had to be captured. But scouts reported that the natural defences were virtually impregnable. And Montcalm, the French general, was assured by his officers 'Only God can do the impossible'. There was, however, a chink in the armour - a rarely used path that wound up to The Heights of Abraham. By night, Wolfe and 1700 men, outwitting French batteries and sentries, slipped silently ashore from an armada of boats, and clawed their way equally silently up to the summit to take the too complacent French unawares.

Not all his 3,000 reinforcements could move like ghosts. French bugles blared. In the desperate counter-attack Wolfe's wrist was shattered by a musket ball . . . a second shot struck him in the chest, slowing him to a staggering walk . . . a third brought him to his knees only half conscious . . . Withering British fire, a bayonet charge, and then the cry 'See, the French run!'. And Wolfe, dying, murmured, 'Now I am contented.' Montcalm too died . . . and the way to Quebec and to British Canada was open.

Wolfe was certainly a hero but he had never looked one: slight, frail; red-headed (though that perhaps was the source of his hot temper and dash,) often wracked with pain, and with what artists considerately dubbed 'an eccentric profile'. Indeed he himself admitted, 'I am a whimsical person'. He soared between exhilaration and depression, was tireless in his duties, though not averse to an occasional bout of dissipation; let self-confidence turn to arrogance, and ardently sought responsibility.

His broken body, swathed in a dressing-gown (which can still be seen at Quebec House) was brought back to England for burial at a Greenwich church. Fittingly it was one dedicated to Saint Alphege, Archbishop of Canterbury, who, alone and old, had defied the Danes as fiercely as Wolfe had attacked the French.

You can see Wolfe still on Westerham's sloping green as, cane in hand, he leads his men into battle; the men of whom Cowper wrote, truthfully if a little pompously: 'All were swift to follow whom all loved'. In those days brass-hats, rashly perhaps, led from the front.

Only a hundred yards from him is another wartime hero, Winston Churchill. But in sad contrast his sculptor has seated him, carpet-slippered, in an armchair! Not giving a triumphant V-sign to Hitler or jauntily waving his hat aloft among blitz rubble. Even so, James Wolfe must be glad to have such a neighbour, a man of his own passionate determination.

ZBOROWSKI, Count Vorow (Died 1902)

Addicted Racing Driver . . .

L IVED spasmodically at Highland Court high on the Downs above Bridge near Canterbury. Could well afford it as his father had left him a little matter of £11,000,000. And left him also the thrill of motor racing in his blood. Left him when his gold cuff-links had caught in the throttle lever as his Daimler plunged over the Grande Corniche at Nice . . .

Vorow made frequent forays to European racing circuits but became ever more interested in Captain J. E. P. Howey's project: building a 15 inch gauge railway across a conveniently flat Romney Marsh. Count Vorow had long flirted with Death. Now he went just one step too far, and was killed on his favourite track at Monza in Italy.

Sad, but undaunted, Howey, at £2,000 a mile, laid the Romney, Hythe and Dymchurch Railway track. He too could well afford it. His grandfather in an Aussie gamble had bought 128 acres of useless scrubland: 'You never know . . .'. But he had not lived to see them become the centre of boomtown Melbourne.

With its superb one-third scale Pacifics, 'Green Goddess' and 'Northern Chief', the R. H. and D. R. has thrilled young and old for nearly 70 years. And played no small part in the construction of PLUTO (qv), the war-time lifeline.

Zborowski's other memorial? Chitty-chitty-bang-bang! The racing car he designed, and Ian Fleming made immortal.